Good Food
From

SWEDEN

HIPPOCRENE INTERNATIONAL COOKBOOK SERIES

The Cuisine of Armenia

A Belgian Cookbook

The Art of Brazilian Cookery

The Best of Czech Cooking

Traditional Recipes of Old England

The Best of Finnish Cooking

The Art of Hungarian Cooking

The Art of Irish Cooking

The Art Israeli Cooking

The Art of Persian Cooking

Old Warsaw Cookbook

The Best of Polish Cooking

Polish Heritage Cookery

Old Polish Traditions in the Kitchen

The Best of Russian Cooking

Traditional Food from Scotland

Traditional South African Cookery

The Art of South American Cookery

A Spanish Family Cookbook

The Best of Smorgasbord Cooking

Good Food from Sweden

The Art of Turkish Cooking

The Best of Ukrainian Cuisine

All Along the Danube

Good Food From

SWEDEN

Inga Norberg

HIPPOCRENE BOOKS
New York

Originally published by
Sweden House, Inc., New York.

Hippocrene paperback edition, 1996.

For information, address:
HIPPOCRENE BOOKS, INC.
171 Madison Ave.
New York, NY 10016

Library of Congress Cataloging-in-Publication Data
Norberg, Inga.
    Good food from Sweden / Inga Norberg. -- Hippocrene
pbk. ed.
        Originally published: New York : Sweden House, 1939.
        Includes index.
        ISBN 0-7818-0486-8
        1. Cookery, Swedish.   I. Title.
    TX722.S8N67   1996
    641.59485--dc20   96-21639
                                                        CIP

Printed in the United States of America.

FOREWORD

The recipes in this book will prove to you that the Swedish housewife is a culinary artist who knows how to turn an inexpensive and simple item on the menu into an appetizing dish by just a few deft touches. She also bears in mind the stimulating effect of a varied menu, as a welcome change from everyday fare. Being also both clever and economical, she realizes the nutritive value of eggs, cream and butter, and would never in her cooking stint an extra egg or pint of cream, knowing that she will get far more real food-value out of those ingredients than out of an equally expensive slice of meat, not to speak of the appetizing effect they will have on an otherwise uninteresting dish.

The Swedish housewife also has a flair for turning to good account the cheaper cuts of meat, which are generally looked down on by the American cook for the simple reason that she has never learnt how to transform them into nourishing and tasty dishes. *I am thinking of minced meat.* Not the kind you buy "ready-made," nor the remains of the Sunday roast, having passed through the usual Monday morning rites. The Swedish minced meat arrives from the butcher in its original state, be it good stewing beef, best forequarter veal, or pork, and the mincing process takes place in her own kitchen. This to ensure that there is no violation of what might be looked upon as the Swedish housewife's golden rule: "Only the best (meaning superior and unimpaired raw materials) is good enough."

There are a few cooking utensils that the Swedish house-wife finds invaluable, and that in the long run would well repay the comparatively small initial outlay. Those utensils can be had from the hardware department of most leading stores.

Finally, I wish to tell you that many American dishes are quite popular in Sweden and that I have noticed how every year an increasing number of American recipes find their way into our Swedish cookery books. Exchange being no robbery, I hope that our American friends will take kindly to these typically Swedish recipes.

INGA NORBERG

CONTENTS

GOOD FOOD
FROM SWEDEN

SANDWICHES AND SNACKS
and
SNACKS FOR THE COCKTAIL PARTY

THREE sandwiches on a small plate, with a sprig of parsley, or a couple of radishes, adding a jolly touch, often takes the place of *hors d'oeuvres* at a Swedish dinner. These sandwiches are placed on the left of each person, and as you sit down at table, the maid puts the plate in front of you. Small glasses of beer are served round on a tray, the glasses being removed before the next course is served.

These sandwiches, or snacks rather, have bread *only for their foundation*. They are about ⅛ inch thick, and are cut either in about 3-inch squares, oblongs, or else shaped into rounds with a pastry cutter. Dark or white bread may be used, or for anchovy snacks, Swedish hard bread, while toast would be most suitable for caviar snacks. These snacks should be well buttered and neatly trimmed. The butter to be unsalted, and creamed, and in some cases mixed with a suspicion of mustard.

Left-over peas and salad make delicious snacks; also ham and tongue, etc. Piped with thick mayonnaise, or covered with a thin layer of aspic, with a star of truffles or carrot underneath, they will be irresistible. What you want more than anything else for these little dainties is imagination, ingenuity and a sense of color.

Striped Sandwiches

A Novel Idea for Tea and Cocktail Parties

1 sandwich loaf (yesterday's)
1 cup butter
½ teaspoon French mustard
3 tablespoons cooked ham
3 tablespoons tongue
3 tablespoons cooked veal
3 tablespoons smoked salmon
1¾ oz. gruyère cheese
1 picked gherkin

Remove crusts. Slice loaf lengthwise. Cream butter with mustard. Spread slices on both sides with butter, top and bottom slices only on one side. Sandwich with one layer each of ham, gruyère, veal, salmon and tongue. Cover veal layer with thinly sliced gherkin. Cover loaf with wax paper, wrap round with cloth, wrung out in cold water. Tie at the ends and in a few places, and press loaf for at least 2 hours between two boards, with not too heavy weight on top.

Cut loaf across in thin slices. Cut each slice in half, straight across, or diagonally, and arrange on plate.

Some of the butter might be dyed green with vegetable color. Alternate layers of dark and white bread is delicious, but the loaves must be the same size and shape. The salmon might be omitted.

Anchovy Snacks

Hardboil eggs. Chop finely. Skin and fillet Swedish anchovies. Spread thin slices of sandwich loaf thinly with butter. Shape into rounds with pastry cutter or glass. Put a fillet round each snack and fill the middle with chopped eggs. Or cut slices into small squares, or fingers. Cut fillets into thin strips and arrange in stripes diagonally across, with chopped eggs in between.

Tomato and Egg Snacks

Hardboil eggs and cut into slices. Slice tomatoes. Spread thin slices of sandwich loaf thinly with butter. Shape into small rounds with a glass or pastry cutter. Put a tomato slice on each, topped with an egg slice. Sprinkle with finely chopped truffles or parsley.

Caviar Snacks

Make sardine paste by removing skin and bones, and mash the fish with a little butter, vinegar, salt and pepper to a smooth consistency. Spread thin slices of white bread thinly with butter, mixed with a little mustard and a few drops of vinegar. Remove crusts and cut into small squares. Pipe sardine paste in stripes diagonally across, with caviar in between.

Cooked kippers might be used instead of the sardines, but will not impart such a delicate flavor.

Swedish Caviar Snacks

Swedish caviar is somewhat similar to "Gentleman's Relish," and can be had from most leading grocers. A little cream mixed with it improves the flavor.

Hardboil eggs, and slice. Remove yolks and chop finely. Spread thin slices of sandwich loaf thinly with butter. Cut into small rounds. Put an egg slice on each, fill the hole with caviar and sprinkle with chopped yolk. Or else put a small round of thinly sliced lemon on the caviar.

Shrimp Snacks

Spread thin slices of sandwich loaf thinly with butter. Remove crusts and cut into small oblongs or squares. Arrange shrimps in diagonal rows. Cream unsalted butter, add a little green vegetable color and pipe in strips in between the rows of shrimps. Sprinkle with finely chopped parsley.

Smoked Salmon Snacks

Spread thin slices of sandwich loaf thinly with butter. Cover with slices of smoked salmon. Cut into small rounds. Cream unsalted butter, add a little green vegetable color and pipe a nice pattern on top.

Smoked Eel Snacks

Swedish smoked eel is delicious and can be had from most leading grocers.
Spread thin slices of sandwich loaf thinly with butter. Cut into rounds. Cover with thin round slice of smoked eel. Put a little scrambled eggs on top. Sprinkle with finely chopped truffles, or parsley.

Cheese Snacks

Spread thin slices of sandwich loaf thinly with creamed unsalted butter, mixed with a very little mustard. Cover with thin slices of gruyère cheese. Remove crusts and cut into small oblongs, triangles or rounds. Arrange rows of thinly sliced radishes across.

SMÖRGÅSBORD
(Cold Cut Buffet)

You are sure to have heard about Swedish *"smörgås-bord,"* or *hors d'oeuvres,* the prelude to a Swedish lunch or dinner. It consists of an infinite variety of little appetizing hot or cold snacks and dishes, generally spread on a separate table, from which you are supposed to help yourself. You eat with these bread, cut in slices, or Swedish hard bread (of which there are many varieties that you can buy from most leading stores). You will find in this book recipes of delicious dark bread that goes well with Swedish *smörgåsbord.* In order to really enjoy the *smörgåsbord* you should start off with *"nubben,"* (aquavit), a Swedish appetizer which can be had from leading wine stores. *Nubben* should be served icy cold in tall cone-shaped glasses.

Nothing in the culinary realm gives more scope for a housewife's inventive genius or sense of economy than a Swedish *smörgåsbord,* besides being invaluable as a means of eking out a meagre meal. All those scraps, left over from yesterday, which would not go round if served alone, besides looking most uninteresting, would by a Swedish housewife be transformed into delicious little morsels and served under the all-disguising name of *smörgåsbord.*

I shall give you an idea of what can be done. A guest has turned up for dinner unexpectedly. Shops are closed. A tin of anchovies comes in handy. Hardboil some eggs. Cut in half. Arrange strips of anchovy fillets crosswise over the egg halves. There you have one item! Now cut very thin slices from the cold roast, garnish with sliced gherkins or cucumber, and in the case of veal, the gravy condensed into a jelly and cut into strips. A sprig of parsley will add a jolly touch to your item No. 2. Slice some cold potatoes, sprinkle with finely chopped parsley and serve with filleted anchovies. Garnished with dill, an aromatic plant appreciated by our grandmothers and still favored by Swedish cooks (see page 178), you will have a dish that no man could resist. New potatoes, cooked in their jackets, and a little cream with the herrings, will make them altogether irresistible. Now make a real "gentleman's relish," with the aid of a few Spanish onions or a little savory with some of those much underrated herring, and as your *pièce de résistance* a Swedish omelette, and your guest will be praising you for having treated him to a right royal feast.

These days, when saving is no longer regarded as meanness, but a thing to be proud of, the housewife, blessed with imagination, will find it a most amusing game trying to work out into how many tempting dishes she can turn those left-over scraps.

In following the recipes appearing in this section, the use of Swedish anchovies and herrings (obtainable at most leading stores) is recommended, in preference to the domestic variety.

Eggs with Anchovies

10 anchovies	3 tablespoons bread-
3 tablespoons butter	crumbs
1 red onion	6 eggs

Tail and behead anchovies and remove bone. Turn in breadcrumbs and arrange in buttered omelette dish. Cover with sliced onion. Bake in moderate oven (385° F) to a nice color. Just before ready, remove from oven and drop in the eggs carefully. Return to oven, and leave until eggs are set. *Serve hot.*

Anchovy Savory

18 anchovies
3 medium raw potatoes
½ tablespoon chopped red
onion

3 tablespoons butter
2 tablespoons bread-
crumbs

For omelette dish: ½ tablespoon butter, 1 tablespoon breadcrumbs.

Skin and fillet anchovies. Soak for an hour and dry.
Peel and slice potatoes. Peel onions and chop finely.

Butter and breadcrumb baking dish. Fill with layers of
potatoes, anchovies and onions, three of potatoes and two
of anchovies. Cover with breadcrumbs and dot with butter. Bake a golden brown in hot oven (425° F).

Anchovy Savory with Cream

Cut Spanish onions into small dice and brown lightly in
butter. Cover bottom of omelette dish with onion dice.
Arrange a layer of skinned filleted anchovies over, and then
a layer of thin raw potato chips. Pour a little cream over
and, if you like, sprinkle with grated cheese. Bake 15–18
minutes in fairly hot oven (400° F). Serve at once.

Swedish Gentleman's Relish

4 eggs
4 anchovies
2 large Spanish onions

2 tablespoons butter
Anchovy liquor

Hardboil and chop eggs. Chop onions and fry lightly
in half of the butter. Skin, bone and chop anchovies, and
add to the onions, stirring. Remove pan from fire and add
the eggs, the rest of the butter and a little anchovy liquor.
After that the mixture must not boil again. Serve in chafing dish.

Pickled Herrings—I

2 salt herrings	$\frac{1}{2}$ teaspoon white pepper
3–4 tablespoons vinegar	2 tablespoons chopped
2 tablespoons sugar	onions

Soak herrings overnight. Fillet and skin and remove all bones. Mix vinegar, pepper and sugar, and pour over herrings. Leave for a few hours. When serving, cut into $\frac{1}{2}$-inch-wide strips, diagonally across, and arrange on a dish, making it still look like a whole fillet. Sprinkle with finely chopped onions.

Pickled Herrings—II

1 large (or 1$\frac{1}{2}$ smaller) salted herring	5 crushed black pepper-corns
4 tablespoons vinegar	1 tablespoon olive oil
4 tablespoons water	2 cloves
1–2 tablespoons sugar	1 red onion

Clean herring and soak overnight (not more than 12 hours). Skin and fillet, removing all bones. Cut each fillet in half. Put into glass jar and pour over all pickle ingredients, except the onion, well mixed. Leave for 5–6 hours. When dishing up, cut into $\frac{1}{2}$-inch strips across, replacing pieces to look like a whole fillet. Garnish with strips of finely chopped onion. Pour over some of the pickle. *Serve with small boiled potatoes.* Dill might be used instead of the onion (see page 178).

Herring Savory—I

2 salted herrings	4 tablespoons cream
2 tablespoons butter	2 teaspoons chopped
$\frac{1}{3}$ cup breadcrumbs	chives

Soak herrings overnight. Skin, fillet and remove all bones. Turn over fillets in breadcrumbs, and arrange in buttered omelette dish, keeping half of the butter for dotting over the herrings. Bake for 5–10 minutes in fairly hot oven (400° F), pour over the cream, and leave in the oven until the herrings are soft. Sprinkle with chopped chives.

Herring Savory—II

2 large salted herrings
4 medium cooked or raw
   potatoes
2 red onions

¼ teaspoon white pepper
4 tablespoons butter
2 tablespoons bread-
   crumbs

For omelette dish: ½ tablespoon butter, 1 tablespoon breadcrumbs.

Skin and fillet herrings. Soak overnight in plenty of water. Rinse and dry. Cut each fillet into 1-inch slices crosswise. Peel potatoes and slice thinly. Peel onions and chop finely.

Butter and breadcrumb baking dish. Fill with layers of potatoes, herrings and onions, three of potatoes and two of herrings, sprinkling onions with pepper. Cover with breadcrumbs and dot with butter. Bake a golden brown in hot oven (425° F).

Herring Salad

1½ salted herrings
4 tablespoons vinegar
½ teaspoon white pepper
1½ tablespoons sugar

1⅓ cups cooked meat	cut
1¼ cups beets	
1⅔ cups cooked	into
potatoes	
1 pickled gherkin	tiny
2 raw apples	dice

For garnishing: 1 hard-boiled egg.

Skin and fillet herrings and soak overnight. Dry and bone well, and cut into tiny dice. Mix lightly with meat, beets, potatoes, gherkin and apples. Add sugar, vinegar and pepper. Pack into mould, rinsed in cold water. Turn out and garnish with white and yolk of egg, chopped separately. *Serve with whipped cream, colored with beet juice or carmine, or with special dressing.*

Mock Oyster Pudding

4–5 medium-size salt soft
  herring roes
⅔ cup breadcrumbs
2 cups milk (or thin
  cream)

6 tablespoons melted
  butter
5 eggs
1 teaspoon sugar
A little nutmeg

For pie-dish: ½ tablespoon butter, 2 tablespoons breadcrumbs.

Rinse roes well and soak for 3 hours. Dry and chop finely. Mix with breadcrumbs, milk, melted butter and well-beaten eggs. Season. Pour into buttered and breadcrumbed baking dish. Bake a golden brown in moderate oven (350° F). *Time:* 30–40 min. *Serve with melted butter.*

Smelts Savory

24 smelts
6 anchovies
½ tablespoon salt

3 tablespoons butter
2 tablespoons bread-
  crumbs

For omelette dish: ½ tablespoon butter, 1 tablespoon breadcrumbs.

Behead and tail smelts, and take out the bone. Rinse well and dry. Sprinkle both sides with salt and leave for a few minutes. Behead, tail and fillet anchovies. Cut each fillet into two strips. Place one on each flattened-out smelt. Roll tightly lengthwise and arrange in buttered and breadcrumbed baking dish. Sprinkle with breadcrumbs and dot with lumps of butter. Bake a golden brown in fairly hot oven (400° F). *Time:* 25–30 min. *Serve hot or cold.*

Pickled Smelts

25–30 smelts	5 black peppercorns
2 teaspoons salt	7 white peppercorns
2½ teaspoons sugar	2 bay-leaves
4 tablespoons vinegar	4 sprigs of dill
1 cup water	

Tail and behead the smelts, remove bone, rinse well, dry and rub with salt and ½ teaspoon sugar mixed. Boil water, vinegar, peppercorns, bay-leaves and 2 teaspoons sugar. Flatten out smelts, roll tightly, pack close together in saucepan, with sprigs of dill between each layer. Pour over pickle and simmer for ½ hour. *Serve cold.*

Pickled smelts are also nice served in aspic. Remove carefully from saucepan and arrange in a mould, rinsed in cold water, with sprigs of dill at the bottom. Soften 1 tablespoon of gelatine in 3 tablespoons cold water. Add to 2 cups boiling stock. Beat white of one egg to a foam and add to stock. Let aspic come to the boil, leave, covered, by the side of the fire for 10 minutes, strain until clear, and pour over the smelts. Leave in cool place to set.

Lobster and Fish in Aspic

3 medium-size lobsters	6 white peppercorns
2 lbs. fish (hake or salmon)	1 bay-leaf
5 cups water	1 tablespoon salt

Aspic:

4½ cups fish stock	½ cup cold water
3 tablespoons gelatine	3 tablespoons white
3 whites of egg	wine

Garnishing: 1 hard-boiled egg, 1 truffle, parsley.

Cook fish in water, with salt and peppercorns. Remove skin and bone. Replace bone in stock and simmer for 20 minutes.

Cut fish and lobster into nice pieces.

To make aspic, soak gelatine in cold water for 10 minutes, put softened gelatine into the stock, also whites, lightly beaten up, and the crushed egg-shells. Boil for 2 minutes, beating well. Cover saucepan and leave by the side of the fire for about ½ hour. Strain through cloth, or napkin, wrung out in hot water. If liquid is not clear, pour back again, and keep on straining until quite clear. When cold, add wine (or a tablespoon brandy).

Cover bottom of a mould, rinsed in cold water, with aspic. When set, arrange sections of hard-boiled eggs, pieces of truffle and sprigs of parsley in a nice pattern. Pour over a few drops aspic and allow to set before adding the fish and the lobster. Arrange the best pieces of lobster at the bottom and around the sides, then fill the mould with the rest of the lobster and the fish. Pour over remaining aspic and put in cool place to set.

Serve with mayonnaise or with cream dressing.

Swedish Scrambled Eggs

Take 2 tablespoons milk to each egg. Beat well eggs, milk, pinch of salt and, if you like, a pinch of sugar. Butter a saucepan with cold butter. Pour in mixture and put over slow fire. As the mixture sets, scoop out gently with a spoon. Some finely chopped parsley, cooked with the mixture, adds a nice flavor.

Serve with Swedish sausage, which is delicious, fried bacon, etc.

Peasant Omelette

3 eggs ¼ lb. smoked bacon
1 cup milk Salt

Dice bacon and put into well-buttered omelette dish. Beat eggs with milk and a little salt and pour over the bacon. Bake a nice color in slow oven (325° F).

Salted salmon or anchovies can be used instead of the bacon.

Plain Swedish Omelette

4 eggs 1 cup milk, or thin cream
¼ teaspoon salt (4 tablespoons for each
¼ teaspoon sugar egg)

For omelette pan: ½ tablespoon butter.

Beat yolks well with salt and sugar. Add milk, then whites, beaten to a froth. Pour into omelette pan, or baking-dish, buttered cold. Bake a nice color in moderate oven (350° F). Do not open the oven door for the first 15 minutes.

If baked in an omelette pan, turn the omelette on to a buttered saucepan cover. Cover one-half of the omelette with a stew, made with lobster, mushrooms, asparagus, shrimps, left-over fish or meat (especially chicken or game), diced, peas or carrots, diced, or even creamed spinach (see page 103), fold over the other half and turn the omelette on to a dish.

If baked in a baking-dish, just pour the stew over the omelette and serve.

Lobster Omelette

5 eggs	Salt
2 cups thin cream	Sugar

Omelette pan: 1 teaspoon butter.

Lobster stew:

1 tablespoon butter	Salt
2 tablespoons flour	White pepper
1¼ cups thin cream	Pinch sugar
Large tin of lobster	1 yolk

Make omelette as described above. Dish up and pour lobster stew over half of it, folding the other half over the stew.

For the stew, melt butter, add flour, stirring well, add milk gradually, stirring over the fire. Cook for 10 minutes, stirring. Remove from fire. Season. Not too much pepper! Add contents of lobster tin, cut into small pieces, using the liquid as well. The stew should have the consistency of a fairly thick white sauce. A raw yolk, added to the stew last of all, gives a nice color and richer flavor. *The stew must not boil after the yolk has been added.*

Mushroom Omelette

Omelette: 5 eggs   Salt
1¼ cups thin cream   (Sugar)
Omelette pan: 1 teaspoon butter.
Mushroom stew:

½–¾ lb. mushrooms, or large   1½ cups milk or thin cream
  tin button mushrooms   (mushroom liquid from
2 tablespoons butter   tin)
4 tablespoons flour   Salt, white pepper
                                     1 yolk

Make omelette as described on page 23.

Mushroom stew: Melt butter in saucepan. Add mushrooms, cleaned, trimmed and cut into pieces. Cook gently for about ½ hour, shaking the pan occasionally. Add flour, stirring. Add milk gradually, stirring, and cook for 10 minutes. Season. Last of all stir in raw yolk, *after which the stew must not boil.*

If tinned mushrooms are used, the 1½ cups liquid needed can be made up from part milk and part mushroom liquid.

Dish up omelette and pour mushroom stew over half of it, folding the other half over the stew.

Asparagus Omelette

5 eggs   Salt
3 cups milk   Pinch of sugar
1 teaspoon flour
Omelette pan: 1 teaspoon butter.
Asparagus stew:

1 tablespoon butter   Tin asparagus tips (about
2 tablespoons flour   1 cup)
1 cup milk (or thin cream   Salt, white pepper
  or liquid from aspara-   Pinch of sugar
  gus)

Omelette: Beat all ingredients well together. Pour into buttered omelette pan and bake a nice color in slow oven (325° F). Turn on to a saucepan cover, and from there to a dish. Pour stew over half of the omelette, folding the other half over the stew.

Asparagus stew: Heat butter, add flour, stirring. Add milk and asparagus liquid gradually, stirring. The stew should have the consistency of a fairly thick white sauce. Cook for 10 minutes. Put in asparagus and season.

Asparagus Soufflé

Soufflé:

2 tablespoons butter	5 eggs
4 tablespoons flour	Salt, white pepper
2 cups thin cream	

Savarin mould: 1½ tablespoons butter, 2 tablespoons bread-crumbs.

Asparagus stew:

½ tablespoon butter	½ cup thin cream
1 tablespoon flour	1 tin asparagus tips

Garnishing: 1 tin ordinary asparagus.

Soufflé: Heat butter, add flour, stirring. Add cream gradually, stirring, and cook for a few minutes, stirring. Remove from fire, and when fairly cool, add yolks, one at a time, and season. Cut into mixture, with a knife, well-beaten whites. Pour into buttered and breadcrumbed savarin mould, and place the mould in a tin of boiling water in moderate oven (385° F). *Time for baking:* about 40 min.

Turn out on a round dish and fill the hole in the middle with asparagus stew.

Arrange heated asparagus around the soufflé. *Serve with Creamed Butter.*

Cheese Soufflé

4 tablespoons butter	1 cup grated cheese
4 tablespoons flour	Salt, white pepper
5 eggs	$\frac{1}{4}$ teaspoon mustard
2 cups milk	$\frac{1}{2}$ teaspoon sugar

Soufflé dish: $\frac{1}{2}$ tablespoon butter, 2 tablespoons bread-crumbs.

Heat butter, add flour, stirring, and cook for 2 minutes. Add boiling milk gradually, stirring, and cook for 5 minutes. Allow to cool slightly. Add yolks, one at a time, and stir for 10 minutes. Add cheese and seasoning, also whites, beaten to a stiff froth. Pour into buttered and breadcrumbed soufflé or baking-dish, and bake in moderate oven (350° F) for about 40 minutes. *Serve at once with Creamed Butter.*

Could also be baked in shells and served as a savory.

CROQUETTES

THIS delicious addition to the *smörgåsbord* can be made from left-over fish, meat, chicken or game. Once you know the secret of croquette-making, it only requires some ingenuity and a few scraps of "left-overs" to turn out a really attractive item for your *hors d'oeuvres*.

Sweetbread Croquettes

½ lb. calf's sweetbreads
1 tin mushrooms (or ½ lb. fresh mushrooms)
2½ tablespoons butter
3 tablespoons flour
4 tablespoons sweetbread stock

4 tablespoons mushroom liquid
¾ cup thin cream
1–2 yolks
½ tablespoon gelatine
Salt, white pepper, pinch of sugar

Coating:

2 tablespoons flour
1 egg

4 tablespoons bread-crumbs
Salt, 1 teaspoon olive oil

Cooking: 1½ lbs. lard.

Soak sweetbreads for one hour in cold water. Blanch, i.e., put on in cold water with ½ teaspoon salt, and let it come to the boil. Cook, uncovered, for 10 minutes, then transfer to a saucepan with 1 pint boiling salted water and cook for 30 minutes. Drain, but keep the stock.

Dice sweetbreads and mushrooms, and fry gently in half of the butter. Heat the remaining butter, add flour, stirring, cook for 2 minutes, stirring, add sweetbread stock,

28

mushroom liquid and cream, stirring, and cook for 5 minutes. Add sweetbreads, mushrooms, gelatine, softened in a tablespoon of cold water, stirring gently. Season. Spread on large buttered dish and cover with wax paper.

When cold, spread on floured board, cut into small portions, turn in flour and shape into little cork-shaped croquettes. Brush with well-beaten egg, mixed with oil and seasoning. Turn in breadcrumbs and leave for one hour. Cook a golden brown in deep fat. Drain on brown paper.

Serve hot with Tomato Sauce, or Mushroom Sauce.

If fresh mushrooms are used, take a good cup of cream for the mixture.

Fish Croquettes

1 cup cooked fish	$\frac{3}{4}$ cup thin cream or milk
4 tablespoons butter	1–2 yolks
5 tablespoons flour	$\frac{1}{2}$ tablespoon gelatine
1 cup fish stock	Salt, white pepper

Coating:

2 tablespoons flour	Salt, 1 teaspoon olive oil
1 egg	4 tablespoons breadcrumbs

Cooking: 1$\frac{1}{2}$ lbs. lard.

Heat butter, add flour and stir over the fire for 2 minutes. Add fish stock and cream gradually, stirring, and cook for 5 minutes. Mix with it the beaten yolks, the fish, cut into tiny dice, and the gelatine which was softened in 2 tablespoons cold water. Season. Spread on large buttered dish and cover with wax paper.

When cold, spread on floured board, divide into equal portions, and form into cork-shaped croquettes. Brush with beaten egg, mixed with oil and salt. Turn in breadcrumbs and leave for one hour. Cook a golden brown in deep fat. Drain on brown paper. *Serve with Lobster Sauce, or Mushroom Sauce.*

Chicken Croquettes with Rice

1 cup cold chicken (boned)	½ tablespoon salt
½ lemon	1 bay-leaf, 2 cloves
1½ cups stock or water	2 tablespoons rice

Coating:

2 tablespoons flour	Salt, white pepper
1 egg	4 tablespoons breadcrumbs
1 teaspoon olive oil	

Sauce:

1½ tablespoons butter	2 yolks
3 tablespoons flour	Salt, white pepper
1½ cups thin cream	Pinch of sugar

Wash rice in warm water. Cook in boiling stock until tender, but it must not break. Strain under cold water, and leave to drain.

Melt butter, add flour, stirring, and cook for 2 minutes. Add cream gradually, stirring, and cook for 5 minutes. Add beaten yolks. Stir in the diced chicken, also the rice. Season. Spread mixture on large buttered dish and cover with wax paper.

When cold, divide into equal portions on floured board, roll each portion in flour, and shape into small cutlets. Brush with well-beaten egg, mixed with oil and seasoning. Turn in breadcrumbs, and leave for one hour. Cook a golden brown in deep fat. Drain on brown paper. If you like you could stick a piece of macaroni, covered with a cutlet-frill, into the thin end of the croquette.

Garnish with parsley and serve, very hot, with peas.

TIMBALE CASES

"Krustader," as they are called in Swedish, are made quite easily, and form a most attractive and delicious item on the *smörgåsbord.* For making the timbale cases you require a special iron, which can be bought at a small cost from the hardware department of most leading stores. These cases will keep for 2–3 weeks in an air-tight tin, but should be heated in the oven before using. They can be filled with the same kind of stews that are used for a Swedish omelette.

Timbale cases can be made with water or cream. Both kinds are quite good.

Timbale Cases Made with Cream

(Will make about 30)

¾ cup flour	8 tablespoons thin cream
¼ teaspoon salt	1–2 yolks
2 teaspoons sugar	1 tablespoon melted butter

For cooking: 1½ lbs. lard.

Sift flour, add seasoning, cream and yolk, beating well. When smooth and glossy, add butter that has been melted and cooled.

Have ready a deep, but not wide, pan with hot deep fat and keep the timbale iron immersed in the same for a while before using it. Otherwise the mixture will not adhere.

Pour mixture into one or two cups, according to the number of timbale shapes on your iron (you can get them

31

with one or two shapes).   Dip the iron into the mixture, but not right up to the top, hold over the fire for a moment to avoid blisters, and immerse into the boiling fat.   When a nice golden-brown color, remove, and trim edges with scissors.   Place upside-down on brown paper to drain.

Dip the iron in the fat and drain before letting it go into the mixture again.

The timbale cases can be filled with stews, made from chicken, game, mushrooms, sweetbread, asparagus, lobster, shrimps, fish, or mixed vegetables.

Timbale Cases Made with Water

(Will make about 50)

2 cups flour
2 cups water
1–2 yolks

$\frac{1}{2}$ teaspoon salt
2 teaspoons sugar
2 teaspoons olive oil

For cooking: 1$\frac{1}{2}$ lbs. lard.

Sift flour, add water, yolk and seasoning, beating well. When smooth and glossy, add olive oil.

Proceed, as described above.

Timbale Cases with Sweetbreads and Truffles

Timbale cases, see page 31.

Filling:

1 cup calf's sweetbreads
2 tablespoons butter
5 tablespoons flour
4 tablespoons sweetbread
   stock

2 cups thin cream (or
   milk)
Salt, white pepper, pinch
   of sugar
1 yolk
2–3 truffles

Blanch sweetbreads, as described on page 28. Drain, but keep stock. Dice and heat in butter, until the latter is quite clear. Press out of saucepan with a spoon, leaving butter. Add flour to butter and cook for 2 minutes, stirring. Add sweetbread stock and cream gradually, stirring. Cook for 5 minutes. The stew should have the consistency of a fairly thick white sauce. Add sweetbreads and finely chopped truffles, and let the stew come to the boil. Season and add the yolk, *after which it must not boil.* Fill timbale cases with the stew and serve hot.

Timbale Cases with Mixed Vegetables

Timbale cases, see page 31.

Filling:

1 bunch young carrots	2 tablespoons butter
1 small cauliflower	5 tablespoons flour
A few beans	2 cups vegetable stock
$\frac{2}{3}$ cup new peas	$\frac{1}{2}$ teaspoon meat extract
12 asparagus tips	$\frac{1}{2}$ teaspoon salt
3 cups water	1 yolk
1 teaspoon sugar	2 tablespoons cream

Clean and trim vegetables. Put on in boiling water with 1 teaspoon sugar. When cooked, drain, keeping the stock. Cut vegetables into small pieces. Heat butter, add flour and cook for 2 minutes, stirring. Add gradually vegetable stock, mixed with meat extract and salt, stirring. Cook for 8 minutes. Add well-beaten yolk and cream, *after which the sauce must not boil.* Add salt to taste. Mix vegetables gently with sauce and fill the heated timbale cases.

Also served as an entrée, or to go with smoked salmon, fried fish, etc.

Timbale Cases with Mushrooms

Timbale cases, see page 31.   Mushroom stew, see page 25.

Timbale Cases with Lobster

Timbale cases, see page 31.   Lobster stew, see page 24.

Timbale Cases with Asparagus

Timbale cases, see page 31.   Asparagus stew, see page 25.

Swedish Onions

1 lb. small Spanish onions   Water
4 tablespoons butter   Salt
1 tablespoon sugar

Peel onions and cook in salted water until almost soft.
Drain.   Brown the butter lightly in a saucepan, put in
onions, sprinkle with sugar, and simmer, covered, until
they are a nice brown color and quite tender.   *Serve hot.*
Also delicious served with steak.

Tiny Meat Balls

1 cup minced raw beef   1 egg
¼ cup minced fat pork   3 tablespoons butter
1 teaspoon finely-chopped   2 tablespoons breadcrumbs
   onion   6 tablespoons water

Have beef and pork ground together three times.
Soak breadcrumbs in water.   Fry onions lightly.   Mix
minced meat with the egg, breadcrumbs and water, in
which they have been soaked, pepper, salt and onions.

Work well into smooth consistency with wooden spoon. Shape into tiny balls and fry in butter. When serving, pour over the butter in which they have been fried.

See also Swedish Meat Balls, page 91.

Stuffed Onions

3 large Spanish onions
¼ cup raw steak
¼ cup veal
3 tablespoons fat pork

1 tablespoon breadcrumbs
1 egg
⅔ cup milk
Salt, white pepper

Frying: 2 tablespoons butter.

Peel onions and parboil. Cut steak, veal and pork into small pieces. Pass three times through the meat-grinder. Soak breadcrumbs in milk. Mix with mince meat, egg and seasoning. Work well into smooth consistency with wooden spoon.

Cut off tops from onions. Scoop out and fill with mince mixture. Replace tops. Heat butter in saucepan. Fry onions until they are soft and the stuffing cooked through. *Serve hot.*

Swedish Sausage

Swedish sausages are delicious. They contain no garlic. The ordinary smoked variety needs no cooking. Then there is a lightly smoked kind, called *Medister* sausage, which is equally good, and most suitable for the *smörgåsbord,* or as a *nachspiel* dish. Cut into ½-inch thick slices, fry lightly in butter and serve with Swedish scrambled eggs. Can also be served with stewed potatoes.

Swedish sausages can be had in most leading stores.

Swedish Eggs

6 hard-boiled eggs	Breadcrumbs
1 lb. sausage meat	White of egg

Shell eggs. Brush with lightly beaten white. Cover with sausage meat. Dip in white. Roll in breadcrumbs. Fry a golden brown in deep fat. Cut in halves lengthwise. *Serve hot.*

Pancake Rissoles

Pancakes:

3 eggs	$\frac{3}{4}$ cup flour
2 cups milk	1 teaspoon salt

Frying: 2 tablespoons butter.

Filling:

1$\frac{1}{4}$ cups cooked meat	1$\frac{1}{4}$ cups meat stock
$\frac{1}{2}$ lb. fresh mushrooms or	1 yolk
medium tin mushrooms	4 tablespoons cream
2 tablespoons butter	Salt, white pepper
4 tablespoons flour	

Frying: 3 tablespoons butter, $\frac{2}{3}$ cup breadcrumbs.

Beat eggs, flour, salt and milk well together and leave for 1 hour.

Dice meat. Dice mushrooms and fry in butter. Press mushrooms out of the pan with a spoon, leaving the butter. Add flour to butter and cook for 2 minutes, stirring. Add stock gradually and cook for 5 minutes, stirring. Beat yolk with cream and add, after which *the sauce must not boil.* Add meat and mushrooms. Season.

Heat pancake pan and brush with butter. Make thin pancakes but fry them only on the one side. Spread pancakes on chopping-board, uncooked side up. Sprinkle with breadcrumbs. Cut in half, and put one tablespoon of meat mixture on each half. Fold nicely into an oblong parcel. Turn gently in breadcrumbs and fry a nice color in butter. Arrange on hot dish, and garnish with parsley. *Serve with melted butter or with Mushroom Sauce.*

The batter can also be made into small pancakes, using a Swedish *"plättpanna"* (pancake pan).

Pytt-I-Panna (Hash)

2 cups left-over meat
3½ cups cooked potatoes
2-3 red onions

4 tablespoons butter
Salt, white pepper

Dice meat (beef or veal with ham or salt beef) and potatoes. Fry finely chopped onions in butter. Add meat, potatoes, and pepper and salt to taste. Not too much! Stir gently over fire, taking care not to mash the mixture. When lightly browned, *serve with pickled beets.* Serves 6.

Served with fried eggs it makes a delicious nachspiel dish, as a change from bacon and eggs or kippers.

Kidnoy Sauté

2 veal kidneys
1 teaspoon salt
¼ teaspoon white pepper
1 tablespoon flour
1 tin mushrooms (about ½ pint)

4 tablespoons butter
⅔ cup brown stock
1½ tablespoon Madeira or Sherry

Blanch kidneys, i.e., put into cold salted water and, when boiling, cook for 2-3 minutes. Drain. When cold, slice, season and turn in flour. Slice mushrooms. Lightly brown butter in saucepan, put in kidneys and mushrooms, and brown evenly, shaking the pan. Add stock and cook for 10 minutes. Add wine and let it come to the boil. *Serve hot.*

Stewed Calf's Brain

1 calf's brain	2 tablespoons cream
2 tablespoons butter	Salt, white pepper, ginger

Wash in several waters and proceed as described on page 26. Drain, but do not keep the stock. When cold, remove all skin and fibres. Chop finely. Heat butter, add brain and fry lightly. Add cream and seasoning. Cook for 10 minutes. *Serve hot, plain, or garnished with small croûtons. (Bread fingers, fried in butter).*

Kalvsylta (Veal Brawn)

2 lbs. neck of veal	1 tablespoon salt
1 meaty knuckle of veal	½ teaspoon white pepper
Water	2 tablespoons vinegar
1 teaspoon gelatine	

Simmer meat in enough cold water to cover, until tender. Take out meat, remove bones and sinews, and put back into the stock, letting it simmer while you chop the meat. Strain the stock and add the meat. Simmer for 10 minutes. Season, add vinegar and, if necessary, 1 teaspoon gelatine, softened in a tablespoon cold water. Leave by the side of the fire for 10 minutes. Pour into moulds, rinsed in cold water. When set, cut in slices. *Serve with pickled beets.*

Pressylta (Swedish Brawn)

1 pig's head (about 9 lbs.)	15 white peppercorns
4–5 lbs. shoulder of veal	Good 3 tablespoons salt
Water	2 bay-leaves
15 black peppercorns	

Seasoning for brawn: 3 tablespoons salt, good 2 teaspoons white pepper.

Split head in two, wash well and soak for 24 hours in plenty of cold water, changing the water twice. Put head and veal in saucepan with boiling water to cover. When water comes to the boil skim well. Add salt, bay-leaves and peppers. Simmer until meat comes easily away from bones. Remove meat from saucepan and cut away rind from pig's head in as large pieces as possible.

When meat has cooled, cut in slices. Spread cloth, or napkin, wrung out in hot water, over the bottom of a large bowl. Arrange pieces of rind on cloth, right side down. Spread with alternate layers of veal and pork, sprinkling pepper and salt on each layer. Cover with pieces of rind. Bind cloth securely with twine, and put brawn into saucepan with stock, on a plate turned upside down. Heat it through. Remove from saucepan and press for 24 hours with weights of about 10 lbs. on top. Remove cloth and keep brawn in strongly salted cold water. *Serve, sliced, with pickled beets.*

Pig's Knuckles

4 pig's knuckles	2 tablespoons salt
8 cups water	$\frac{1}{4}$ teaspoon soda

Soak knuckles for 24 hours in plenty of cold water. Scald in hot water and scrape well. Put on in cold water with soda. When water boils, skim, and go on cooking until the meat is tender. Remove from stock, steep at once in cold salted water, to give them a good color. Serve cold in some of the stock, which will have turned into jelly. *Delicious with pickled beets.*

Pig's Knuckles

(Another Way)

4 pig's knuckles	2 tablespoons salt
3 quarts water	¼ teaspoon soda

Coating and frying:

1 egg	⅔ cup breadcrumbs
3 tablespoons butter	

Cook knuckles as described above. When cooked, split lengthwise and remove bone. Press between two boards until cold. Brush over with beaten egg and turn in breadcrumbs. Fry a nice golden brown in butter. *Serve with fried potatoes.*

Stuffed Tomatoes

6 nice large tomatoes	Salt, white pepper
1 tin mushrooms	2 tablespoons grated cheese
1½ tablespoons butter	1 tablespoon melted butter

Dip tomatoes in hot water, skin, cut in two, and remove some of the pulp with a teaspoon. Chop mushrooms finely and fry in the butter until it is clear. Press them out of the saucepan with a spoon and mix with the thickest part of the tomato pulp. Season, and fill the scooped-out tomatoes with the mixture. Arrange in baking-dish, sprinkle with grated cheese and pour over some melted butter. Bake in hot oven (450° F) until they are soft, and the stuffing is a nice golden brown. Serve at once.

Also very nice served with fried meat.

Liver Paste

1¼ lb. calf's liver	4 teaspoons anchovy liquid
4 tablespoons breadcrumbs	2 teaspoons salt
4 eggs	2 teaspoons sugar
1 cup thin cream	½ teaspoon white pepper
½ cup fat pork	¼ teaspoon ground cloves
½ cup veal	Pinch of ground nutmeg

For tin: 1 cup fat pork.

Rinse liver and leave in water for 15 minutes. Soak breadcrumbs in cream, mixed with beaten eggs. Cut pork fat into tiny dice. Dry liver and cut into pieces, also the veal. Mince 4 times. Pound in mortar and pass through wire sieve. Mix mince with pork dice, add gradually cream with eggs, condiments and anchovy liquid. Line a tin with thin slices of fat pork, fill with paste, cover well with greased paper and steam slowly for about 2 hours. When cold, cut in thin slices, and serve on the *smörgåsbord*.

Spinach Soufflé

3 tablespoons butter	4 egg yolks and 4 whites
½ cup flour	¾ lb. spinach
2¼ cups milk	Salt and pepper

Garnishing: 4 hard-boiled eggs.

Cook and chop the spinach very fine. Make a cream sauce of butter, flour and milk. Season and add the yolks, beating vigorously until light and cool. Add the spinach and fold in the whites. Pour the mixture into a well greased baking-dish. Bake in moderate oven (385° F) for about 45 minutes in shallow pan with water. Allow to stand for a few minutes before unmoulding. *Serve with*

Hollandaise sauce, as a separate dish or on the smörgås-bord, garnished with the hard-boiled eggs. Serves 6.

Stuffed Eggplant

3 eggplants
2 tablespoons butter
½ cup cooked rice
½ teaspoon salt
3 hard-boiled eggs

½ teaspoon pepper
½ cup breadcrumbs
(1 cup minced meat)
½ teaspoon sugar

Cut the eggplants in halves and cook for a few minutes in salted water. Remove the pulp carefully and mix with eggs, rice, butter, seasoning and meat if desired. Fill the shells with the combination and cover the tops with bread-crumbs and small dabs of butter. Bake in hot oven (425° F) until brown and eggplant is tender. *Serve as a separate course or for Sunday night supper.* Serves 6.

Steamed Spare Ribs

3 lbs. spare ribs
½ teaspoon pepper
1 tablespoon salt
6 medium apples

1 tablespoon sugar
1 cup prunes
2 cups boiling water

Wipe the meat with cloth wrung in hot water and rub the meaty side with salt and pepper. Spread ribs with the bony side up and cover with prunes and slices of apples dipped in sugar. Make roll and tie securely to retain the fruit inside the package. Brown in butter and remove to kettle. Add water, cover well and let it steam for about 2 hours. Cut in attractive pieces and serve on hot platter, garnished with the fruit. *It is delicious cold with cocktails or as an attractive addition on the smörgåsbord.* Serves 6.

Salmon in Aspic

3 lbs. salmon
1½ tablespoons salt
3 sprigs dill

8 whole peppercorns
4 cups water
2 tablespoons vinegar

Cut salmon in attractive pieces and let them boil in water with above ingredients until done. Remove to aspic-dish and prepare the aspic by taking 3 cups stock, 2 tablespoons gelatine, white of one egg and let it boil for a few minutes. Strain and pour over fish. Leave in cool place a few hours until stiff. Unmould and garnish with parsley or dill. A delicious summer dish as well as a welcome part of the *smörgåsbord*.

It the salmon is to be served whole, allow about 45 minutes for cooking. Do not let the fish cook to pieces. Prepare aspic as above, and when about to jell, drop by spoonfuls slowly on the fish and let it stiffen in cold place. *Serve with mayonnaise or a sharp sauce.* Serves 6.

Mackerel with Dill

3½ lbs. fresh mackerel
1½ tablespoons salt
2 sprigs dill

1 bay-leaf
4 cups water
3 tablespoons vinegar

Clean, wash and cut the fish in three or four pieces crosswise. Rub with salt and vinegar and let it stand for about an hour. Cook slowly in seasoned water for about ten minutes. When done, remove and serve in its own liquid.

As a summer dish prepare aspic according to recipe given on page 65, and serve with horseradish sauce or other sharp sauce. Serves 6.

Lobster Pilaff

2–3 lobsters	butter
1 tablespoon butter	stock
1 cup wine (white)	cayenne pepper
1 tablespoon brandy	1 tablespoon parsley
¼ cup oil	1 teaspoon salt
1 tomato, cut	

Rice: 1 cup rice, 3 cups light stock.

Cut lobster open with sharp knife and remove stomach and intestines. Heat oil and butter in frying pan and let lobsters simmer in fat, sprinkled with salt, until shells turn red. Add wine, brandy and tomato, cover and let it cook *slowly* for about 20 minutes.

Remove meat from lobsters and cube. Strain pan juice into small saucepan, add dabs of butter and rich stock, season to taste. Add lobster meat and heat.

Boil rice in stock and season (onion if desired). Pile on platter and flatten top. Pour lobster-mixture over and serve very hot. Serves 6.

Jellied Lobster

5 cooked lobsters	1 head of lettuce, shredded
2½ cups mayonnaise	1 stalk of celery, cut very fine
1 small can peas	
1 small can asparagus, diced	

Aspic: 3 cups fish stock, 2 tablespoons gelatine, 1 egg white, 1 teaspoon brandy.

Cook and chill lobsters and cut lengthwise. Remove meat in big pieces and slice. Remove the claws whole. Mix salad ingredients with most of mayonnaise and fill the cleaned shells. Spread tops with mayonnaise and an attractive piece of lobstermeat in the center.

Prepare aspic according to recipe on page 65. When it begins to thicken, pour carefully over the salad as a coating. Arrange the rest of the salad in the center of large platter, spread with mayonnaise, coat with aspic. Garnish with meat from the claws. Place shells on lettuce leaves around the salad. Chill thoroughly before serving. *An ideal summer dish and very decorative on smörgåsbord.* Serves 10.

SOUPS

SWEDISH soups have a reputation for being delicious. It is not so much a matter of actual ingredients but the fact that the Swedish cook has a natural gift for adding just that pinch of salt or pepper that will make all the difference to a soup or a sauce. But remember that it is better erring on the mean side when it comes to seasoning. Also that a pinch of salt to a sweet dish will often mean as great an improvement as a pinch of sugar to most other dishes.

In addition to ordinary soups the Swedish housewife treats her family to sweet milk soups and fruit soups, both of which take the place of puddings. They may not appeal to an ordinary palate, but being both tasty and nourishing, and easily assimilated, they can be well recommended for children and invalids.

All thick soups and milk soups should be well beaten up just before serving. A small lump of butter, added to the latter ones at the last moment, makes them nice and creamy.

Vegetable Soup

$\frac{1}{4}$ root celery
1 small onion
1 lb. artichokes
1 small cauliflower
Small bunch parsley
1 cup fresh peas
Salted water
1 tablespoon butter

3 tablespoons flour
$5\frac{1}{2}$ cups mixed beef and
  veal stock
$\frac{1}{2}$ lb. spinach
Salt, white pepper
4 tablespoons cream
2 yolks

46

Clean and trim celery, onion and artichokes and cook them whole in salted water. Boil cauliflower, parsley and peas in salted water in another saucepan. Heat butter, add flour, stirring over the fire. Add boiling stock gradually, stirring. Add picked and rinsed spinach, and cook for 10 minutes. Add artichokes and the two lots of vegetable stock, but leave out celery and onion.

Beat up yolks with cream in soup tureen. Pour the soup over, beating well. Put in peas and cauliflower, cut into pieces. Serves 5.

Vegetable Soup Made with Milk

2 carrots	4 tablespoons butter
1 parsnip	$3\frac{1}{2}$ cups boiling water
$\frac{1}{2}$ root celery	3 tablespoons flour
1 small onion	$3\frac{1}{2}$ cups milk
1 small cauliflower	2 teaspoons salt
$\frac{2}{3}$ cup shelled peas	Sugar
$\frac{1}{4}$ lb. spinach	White pepper
1 tablespoon fine-chopped parsley	2 yolks
	4 tablespoons cream

Clean, trim and dice carrots, parsnip and celery. Cut onion into thin strips. Trim cauliflower, cut into sections and soak in water with a little vinegar for 1 hour.

Fry carrots, parsnip and celery in $1\frac{1}{2}$ tablespoons butter, put on in salted boiling water and cook until half done. Add peas and cauliflower and cook until tender. Transfer vegetables to the soup tureen, keeping the stock. Heat $1\frac{1}{2}$ tablespoons butter, add flour, stirring, cook for 2 minutes, add vegetable stock and boiled milk gradually, stirring over the fire. Add rinsed and coarsely chopped spinach, and cook, stirring, for 5 minutes. Add parsley and seasoning. Remove saucepan from the fire.

Beat yolks and cream, pour into the soup, beating well. Add 1 tablespoon butter to the vegetables in soup tureen, and pour soup over. Serves 6.

Artichoke Soup

2 lbs. Jerusalem artichokes	White pepper
9 cups stock	½ teaspoon sugar
1 tablespoon butter	1–2 yolks
2 tablespoons flour	4 tablespoons cream
Salt	

Wash and trim artichokes. Boil in stock until tender. Pass through wire sieve. Melt butter, add flour, stirring, then the soup gradually, stirring. Simmer for 10–15 minutes. Skim well and season. A little Madeira or Sherry will greatly improve the flavor.

Beat yolk and cream in soup tureen. Pour soup over, beating well. *Serve with small Artichokes, or Croûtons.* Serves 6.

Asparagus Soup

1 lb. asparagus	White pepper
1 tablespoon butter	Pinch of sugar
2 tablespoons flour	1–2 yolks
7 cups rich stock	4 tablespoons cream
Salt	

Cut off asparagus heads and put aside. Trim stalks and cook for a few minutes in slightly salted water. Drain. Melt butter, add flour, stirring, then half of the stock, gradually, stirring. Put in asparagus stalks and simmer until tender. Pass through wire sieve. Add remaining stock and let it come to the boil. Season. Cook asparagus heads until tender in slightly salted boiling water.

Beat yolk and cream in soup tureen. Put in asparagus heads. Pour over soup, beating well. *Serve with plain Croûtons.* Serves 6.

If tinned asparagus is used, heat only the tin in boiling water.

Soup à la Madrilaine

6 medium-size tomatoes	2 tablespoons tapioca
2 tablespoons butter	Salt, white pepper to taste
3 pickled onions	1–2 tablespoons Sherry or
7 cups stock	Madeira

Brown onions lightly in butter. Add coarsely cut tomatoes, also 2 cups of stock. Boil for about 20 minutes. Pass through wire sieve. Cook the remaining stock with tapioca for about 15 minutes. Strain. Add the soup, let it come to the boil, season and add wine. *Serve with Croûtons.* Serves 6.

Nettle Soup

7 cups very young nettles	7 cups rich stock
A few sprigs chives	Pepper, salt to taste
5 tablespoons flour	Pinch of sugar
2 tablespoons butter	

Clean and rinse nettles well. Simmer in boiling, slightly salted water for 15 minutes. Drain nettles and rinse in cold water, then drain again. Chop finely, or pass through wire sieve, together with the chives or dill. Sprinkle with flour. Heat in melted butter, add stock gradually, stirring. Simmer, covered, for three-quarters of an hour. Skim well and season. *Serve with poached eggs or hard-boiled eggs, cut into sections.*

Small lumps of butter, dotted over the soup, when ready, imparts a rich flavor, but it must not boil after the butter has been added.

If there are not enough nettles, eke out with spinach, treated in the same way. Serves 6.

Nettles are picked in the spring. Dry in open air and keep in paper bags, and you will get nettle soup the year round. If nettles are not available, spinach or dandelion greens make a fine substitute.

Emperor Soup

1 tablespoon butter	4 tablespoons Sherry or
3 tablespoons flour	Madeira
7 cups rich stock	2 yolks
Salt, pepper	4 tablespoons cream

Melt butter, add flour, stirring for 2 minutes. Add boiling stock gradually, stirring. Cook for 15 minutes. Season and add wine.

Put well beaten yolks and cream in soup tureen. Pour over soup, beating well. *Serve hot with Egg Balls or hard-boiled eggs, cut in half lengthwise.* Serves 6.

Oxtail Soup

1 oxtail	10 black peppercorns
2 tablespoons butter	1½ tablespoons flour
1 small red onion	7 cups stock
1 small carrot	White pepper, salt
3 sprigs of parsley	3 tablespoons Sherry

Wash tail in hot water and dry well. Cut into small joints. Brown the butter in saucepan. Put in oxtail, peeled onion, scraped and diced carrot, parsley and peppercorns. Simmer for 1–2 hours, stirring fairly often. When a nice brown, add flour mixed with cold water, and leave on for another ½ hour. Add stock gradually, stirring, and cook until meat is quite tender. Strain and skim well. Season and add wine. *Serve with pieces of tail.* Serves 6.

Mock Turtle Soup

1 calf's head	1 tablespoon butter
2 teaspoons salt	3 tablespoons flour
½ teaspoon white pepper	7 cups veal or beef stock
1 small piece ginger	Pinch of cayenne pepper
2 red onions	Browning
2 carrots	2 tablespoons Sherry or
1 celery root	Madeira

Cut head in half, take out the brains, rinse well and soak in cold water for about 12 hours. Put into saucepan, cover with cold water, add salt and, when boiling, skim well. Season and add carrots and celery. Simmer until the bones can be easily removed. Take from saucepan and strain stock. Bone the head and when quite cold, dice the meat.

Peel onions, chop finely and brown in the butter. Add flour, stirring, then the stock gradually, stirring, and cook for 10–15 minutes. Season with cayenne pepper and add wine. *Serve with the meat.* Serves 6.

Black Soup

The 11th November (Mårten Gås) is the day of Goosie Gander in Sweden, when he himself, or his wife, will turn up on practically every dinner table in Sweden, accompanied by that dubious (from any but a Swedish culinary point of view) delicacy *"Black Soup."* Shutting your eyes to the actual making of that particular soup, you will probably in time, and with some experience, turn quite friendly towards the same. Which is only right, considering that it really might be looked upon as a *pièce de résistance des gourmets.* Here is the recipe:

Giblets of 1 goose (neck, heart, gizzard, liver and wing-tips)	3 tablespoons flour
	9 cups stock (including giblet stock)
2 cups goose or pig's blood	6 tablespoons vinegar
1 teaspoon white pepper	1½ lbs. fresh (or 2 oz. dried)
1 teaspoon ground ginger	apples
10 ground cloves	2–3 cups prunes
3 teaspoons salt	2 tablespoons Port or
8 tablespoons sugar	Madeira

Scald giblets, rinse well and leave overnight in cold water. Put aside skin from the neck and the liver, to be used for the goose liver sausage. Put on the rest of the giblets in cold water, and boil until tender. Remove, cut in pieces, and put into soup tureen. Strain stock and skim carefully.

Cook separately, in a little water, peeled apple sections, also previously rinsed and soaked prunes.

Strain blood and beat vigorously. Add flour mixed with 2 cups of cold stock. Let the rest of the stock come to the boil, add blood, beating vigorously until soup has boiled for 10 minutes. Add fruit and fruit liquid, also wine. Season. *Serve hot with Goose Liver Sausage.* Serves 10.

Swedish Pea Soup (Ärter Med Fläsk)

Ärter Med Fläsk might be looked upon as a Swedish national dish. It is served every Thursday at the King's table, as well as at that of his most humble subject. It is actually King Gustaf's favorite dish. Some people drink with the pea soup a glass of hot *"Punsch,"* a famous Swedish liqueur, and it is always followed by pancakes (*Plättar*) or waffles.

2 cups yellow peas
6 cups water
1 lb. pork (fresh, or slightly cured)

2 teaspoons salt
$\frac{1}{4}$ teaspoon ginger

Rinse peas and soak overnight. Put on in cold water, let it come to the boil slowly, then cook vigorously for the first hour, to make the skins come off more easily. As skins float to the surface skim them off. Put in the pork when peas have cooked for 1 hour, and simmer for another 2 hours or so. Season. Cut pork in slices and serve separately with the soup.

If the water is hard, add $\frac{1}{4}$ teaspoon of soda, or else boil water and let it cool again before using it.

Left-over peasoup is very good made into a purée (see recipe following). Serves 6.

Purée of Peas

3 cups left-over pea soup
1½ teaspoons meat extract
5 cups boiling water
2 tablespoons butter

3 tablespoons flour
Salt, white pepper
1 yolk

Heat pea soup and pass through sieve. Add meat extract, dissolved in $\frac{1}{2}$ cupful of the boiling water. Add the rest of the water, and salt to taste. Boil for a couple of minutes. Heat butter, add flour, stirring, add soup gradually, stirring, and cook for 8 minutes. Season. Beat up yolk in soup tureen. Pour over purée, beating well. *Serve with plain Croûtons.* Serves 6.

Swedish Fish Soup

1½ quarts fish bouillon
1 carrot
6 stalks of celery
2 tablespoons chopped
  parsley
10 peppercorns
3 cloves

1 bay-leaf
1 tablespoon butter
3 tablespoons flour
Salt
2 yolks
3 tablespoons grated cheese

The vegetables are put on with the liquid and spices and left to simmer for one hour and a half. Strain and thicken in the usual manner. The cheese is added last before pouring the soup over the beaten yolks and served very hot. Pieces of fish may be left in for garnish. Serves 6.

Cheese Soup

2 tablespoons butter
2½ tablespoons flour
2½ quarts stock, or meat extract diluted with water
Salt, paprika
Madeira

1 yolk
¾ cup cream
About 1 cup grated cheese
Egg Balls or
Cooked egg

Melt butter, add flour. Cook two minutes while stirring. Add stock gradually, stirring, and cook a few minutes, season and add Madeira if desired. Before serving pour the hot soup over the stiffly beaten yolk with cream and cheese and serve very hot. Garnish with Egg Balls or sliced eggs. *Very tasty and appetizing.* Serves 6.

Soup à la Moliere

1 small bunch asparagus or can of tips	1 tablespoon butter
	1 tablespoon flour
1¼ cups green peas, cooked	Cooked veal or chicken
½ cup spinach	2 yolks
About 1½ quarts chicken or veal stock	½ cup of cream
	Salt

Peas and spinach should be cooked in stock and forced through sieve. Thicken with butter and flour creamed together while stirring continuously. The soup should be light green in color and not too thick. Season to taste. For richer soup add the cream and egg yolk. Garnish with asparagus tips and cubes of chicken or veal. Serves 6.

Cream of Chicken Soup

1 stewing chicken	1¾ quarts stock from chicken
Soup vegetables, cubed	Salt, paprika
2 tablespoons butter	Madeira
3 tablespoons flour	1 yolk
Lemon	¾ cup thick cream
Breast meat of chicken	

Cut chicken into small pieces for boiling, rub with lemon, cover with water. Bring to a boil, skim, adding the vegetables and let it simmer for 5–6 hours. Strain stock and let it stand over night. Let the breast meat stay under press.

Remove the rest of the meat and rub it through a sieve. Add one tablespoon butter to each pound of meat. Put beaten yolk and cream in soup tureen. Add all ingredients to soup and heat before pouring it over the beaten cream and yolk. It should have a light yellow color and be served rather thin. Garnish with cubes of the white meat. Serves 6.

Oats Soup

$\frac{2}{3}$ cup ordinary oats
5 cups water
$3\frac{1}{2}$ cups milk

18 prunes, or $\frac{2}{3}$ cup raisins
Sugar, salt to taste
10 almonds

Rinse oats, put on in cold water and simmer, covered, until soft (about 2 hours). Rinse prunes, or raisins, put on in cold water and simmer until soft. Pass oats through wire sieve. Boil milk, add to the oats and let soup come to the boil. Blanch almonds and cut into strips. Add, together with prunes and the water in which they have been cooked. Season and *serve hot*. Serves 6.

Egg-Milk

(For Invalids and Children)

7 cups milk
3 eggs

Sugar, salt to taste
Grated rind of $\frac{1}{4}$ lemon

Separate yolks and whites. Put yolks into soup tureen, and beat whites stiffly. Boil milk, place saucepan by the side of fire and put in with a spoon lumps of white. Take them out again after a couple of minutes and drain on hair sieve. Season milk and pour over the well-beaten yolks in the soup tureen. Put the "islands" on top and sprinkle with granulated sugar. Serves 6.

Chocolate Soup

$\frac{1}{4}$ lb. bitter chocolate
7 cups milk
$\frac{1}{3}$ cup sugar

2 teaspoons potato flour
1 cup cream

Boil milk, break chocolate into small pieces and add. Stir milk over the fire until the chocolate has melted. Add sugar and potato flour mixed in a little cold water. Let soup come to the boil and cook for a couple of minutes. *Serve hot with whipped cream.* Serves 6.

Apple Soup

6 medium fairly sour apples
1½ cups dried apples
7 cups water
Finely-peeled rind of
   ¼ lemon
(Small piece cinnamon)

⅔ cup sugar
1½-2 tablespoons potato
   flour
Lemon juice, or 3 table-
   spoons white wine or
   Madeira

Rinse and dry apples. Core and cut into sections. Cook in boiling water with lemon peel (and cinnamon). When tender, pass through wire sieve. Heat soup with sugar. When boiling, add potato flour, mixed with ½ cup cold water. Cook for 10 minutes, stirring. Add wine, or lemon juice, and more sugar, if wanted. *Serve cold with Whipped Cream and Rusks.* Serves 6.

Wine Soup

(For Invalids)

5 cups water
1 lemon
⅔ cup sugar

1½ tablespoons potato flour
4 yolks
1 cup white wine

Boil water for 15 minutes with finely peeled lemon rind, lemon juice and sugar, leaving out 2 tablespoonfuls of sugar. Remove lemon rind and let it come to the boil again, add potato flour, mixed with wine. Beat yolks with sugar in soup tureen, pour over the soup gradually, while beating. *Serve frothy, with macaroons.*

Hip Soup

2 cups dried hips
9 cups water
1 cup sugar

1½ tablespoons potato
    flour
¼ cup almonds

Rinse hips, put on in cold water and cook until tender (about 2 hours), beating well now and again. Pass through wire sieve, add sugar and potato flour, mixed with a little cold water. Let it come to the boil again. Add more sugar, if wanted. *Serve hot or cold with blanched almonds, cut into strips, and whipped cream.*

Rhubarb Soup

1 lb. rhubarb, cut in pieces
2 quarts water
¾ cup thick cream

1½ tablespoons cornstarch
Sugar to taste
1 yolk

Cook rhubarb until soft. If still young leave the pieces whole. If old, force it through a sieve. Sweeten to taste and add cornstarch, mixed with cold water. Stir until clear while it slowly simmers. Then beat into whipped cream combined with the egg yolk. Serve at once with cookies or cake. Serves 8.

Clabbered Milk Filbunke

5 cups milk

3 tablespoons sour cream

Smear the bottom of 6 glass or, preferably, earthenware bowls, with sour cream. Put the bowls on a shelf in a warm place, pour in the milk, cover with paper or muslin to keep out the dust, and leave until the milk has set and turned sour. *Serve icy cold.* Sprinkle generously with granulated sugar (and a little ginger, if you like).   Most health-giving!

In Sweden *filbunke* is often served with pounded hard bread or ginger nuts.

The milk used for *filbunke* must contain no preservative whatsoever.   Serves 6.

GARNISHERS FOR SOUPS

A SOUP in itself might be rather uninteresting, but even the simplest addition, such as a buttered biscuit with a slice of Roquefort cheese, will spell a nice change. Here are a few delicious additions to your soup. They are easy to make and quite inexpensive.

Cheese Croûtons

White bread
$3\frac{1}{2}$ tablespoons butter

1 white of egg
$\frac{1}{2}$ cup grated cheese

Cut 12 rounds from fairly thin slices of bread. Butter them on one side. Beat egg whites to a froth, mix with Parmesan or other strong cheese, and spread rounds with mixture. Arrange on buttered tin. Just before serving, bake quickly in hot oven (450° F).

Serve with clear and thick soups.

White of an egg can be left out, in which case mix cheese with butter, and spread on rounds.

Potato Croûtons

$\frac{1}{2}$ cup butter
1 cup flour

1 cup cooked grated
   potatoes
1 egg

Coating:
1 yolk
$\frac{1}{2}$ teaspoon salt

1 teaspoon caraway
   seeds

Mix all ingredients well on pastry board. Roll into
lengths, thick as a finger, cut into pieces 2 inches long and
½ inch wide. Brush over with lightly beaten yolk. Sprinkle
with salt and caraway seeds and bake in moderate oven
(385° F).

Serve with consommé or thick soups.

Anchovy Croûtons

| White bread | 9 anchovies |
| ¼ cup butter | 1 white of egg |

Cut fairly thin slices of bread into squares and spread
with butter. Skin and fillet Swedish anchovies, removing
all bones. Put three fillets diagonally across each square,
brush over with lightly beaten white and bake a nice
golden brown in fairly slow oven (325° F).

Generally served with vegetable soups.

Plain Croûtons

| White bread | 2 tablespoons butter |

Cut about one-quarter of a small loaf into tiny dice.
Heat butter in frying pan, put in the bread and shake
pan over the fire until the dice are a nice golden brown.

Serve with purées and other thick soups.

Egg Balls

| 2 eggs | 2 tablespoons butter |

Boil eggs for 10 minutes, leave for a few minutes in cold
water to make the shells come off easily. Remove shells,
and leave eggs until cold. Separate yolks from whites.

Chop yolks finely and mix well with butter. Leave in cold place to get hard. Shape into little balls with two teaspoons, dipped in water. Arrange in a pyramid on a small dish. *Serve with thick soups.*

The balls could be rolled in chopped truffles. The whites might be cut into strips and served in the soup.

Cheese Biscuits

Shortcrust:

1 cup butter	2 tablespoons sugar
1 yolk	2 cups flour

Cheese mixture: ½ cup butter, 1½ cups fairly strong grated cheese.

Wash butter, remove all water, and stir for 5 minutes. Stir yolk and sugar for 10 minutes, add butter and flour and work into smooth and elastic consistency. Leave in cold place for 2 hours. Roll out into about ⅙ inch thickness. Shape with round pastry cutter, and bake a nice golden brown in hot oven (450° F).

To make cheese mixture, stir butter and cheese until light and creamy. Spread on one biscuit, and put another one on top.

Two drops of green coloring, added to the mixture, will make it look nice.

Serve with clear soups.

Potato Patties

Patties:

$\frac{1}{3}$ cup grated cold potatoes $\frac{1}{2}$ cup flour
4 tablespoons butter

Filling:

12 almonds   4 tablespoons cream
2 teaspoons granulated $\frac{1}{2}$ teaspoon flour
  sugar   1 egg

Mix potatoes, butter and flour into smooth paste, and line deep buttered patty tins, keeping a very little paste to cut into thin strips for the tops of the patties.

Stir blanched and grated almonds with sugar and a little of the cream, add egg, flour and the rest of the cream, and work into smooth paste. Fill patty tins with the mixture, and put two strips of the potato paste in a cross on top. Bake in hot oven (425° F). Just before they are ready brush over with lightly beaten egg, to give them a nice color.

Serve with consommé.

Cheese Beignet

3 tablespoons butter $\frac{1}{2}$ cup grated cheese
$\frac{1}{2}$ cup flour   2 eggs
4 tablespoons water

Melt butter, add flour, stirring over the fire. Add water gradually, stirring well. Cook until mixture comes away from the pan (at least 10 minutes). When cool, add eggs, one at a time, also cheese, stirring well. Shape into little balls. Cook a golden brown in deep fat. Drain on brown paper.

Serve with clear soups.

Goose Liver Sausage

2 tablespoons rice
1 cup milk
1 goose liver
1 tablespoon cooked raisins
¼ teaspoon marjoram
¼ teaspoon white pepper

1 teaspoon salt
½ tablespoon fine-chopped onion
½ tablespoon butter
1 yolk

Scald rice, cook in boiling milk until soft and leave to cool. Pound liver, pass through wire sieve and mix with scalded raisins, seasoning and lightly browned onion. Stir in yolk (or a small egg).

Roll off the skin from the neck of the goose, before roasting, clean well and sew up at one end. Stuff three-quarters of the skin with sausage-meat, sew up and simmer, uncovered, for ½ hour, together with the giblets, in salted water.

When cold, cut in slices. *Serve with Black Soup.*

FISH

In Sweden we have practically the same kinds of fish as in America. It is generally cooked in the same way, but whereas an American housewife very often is content to have it served with anaemic-tasting parsley or anchovy sauce, her Swedish prototype uses more imagination and goes to a little more trouble in devising the accompaniment even to the more inexpensive varieties of fish.

I must say that a good grilled or fried American sole takes a lot of beating, but I have also sampled the American boarding-house variety! In Sweden we generally fry our fish in butter. If you will try the idea, be sure to serve on a hot dish, squeeze some lemon juice over, garnish with coarsely chopped parsley that has been boiled for a few minutes in a little salted water, and just before serving pour over a little browned butter.

How to Make Aspic

In order to add an attractive touch to left-overs, meat and fish alike may be moulded in aspic or covered with a glazed coating to prevent drying or discoloration. As a general rule use the seasoned stock, clear with an egg white and stiffen with gelatine, softened in 3 tablespoons of cold water. Flavor with sherry, brandy or vinegar. Combine the ingredients and let it cook for a couple of minutes. Leave it by the side of the stove for some ten minutes before straining through a woven cloth or flannel.

Use for each quart of stock 2½ tablespoons gelatine, 2 egg whites and two tablespoons flavoring.

Aspic used for garnishing must be stiffer, so in that case use 3½ tablespoons gelatine and let it stiffen in a shallow pan. The cutting or dicing should be done with a sharp knife, dipped in hot water.

Smoked Salmon with Spinach

12 slices of smoked salmon	6 poached eggs
Sprigs of dill (or parsley)	1½ cups stock, milk or water
1½ lbs. spinach	½ tablespoon sugar
2 tablespoons butter	1½ teaspoon salt
3 tablespoons flour	

Cook spinach as described on page 103.

Fold slices of salmon double and arrange in a row along the middle of a dish. Surround by spinach and poached eggs. *Serve with spinach.* Serves 6.

Pickled Salmon (Gravlax)

Gravlax is a Swedish "Gentleman's relish" and much appreciated by Scandinavian *gourmets*. It may, or it may not, appeal to the American palate, but it is worth trying. Here is the recipe:

About 4 lbs. salmon	½ teaspoon coarsely pounded
2 tablespoons salt	white peppercorns
Pinch of saltpetre	Sprigs of dill
2 teaspoons sugar	

Cut from a 7–8 pound salmon a piece in the middle, weighing about 4 lbs. Clean and scrape well, carefully removing the bone, and divide into two equal pieces. Wipe

with cloth, wrung out in cold water. Sprinkle with a mixture of sugar and finely pounded salt and saltpetre, rub-
bing it in lightly. Pepper and a few sprigs of dill might
be added, but is not necessary. Put the two pieces together,
with the thick part of one against the thin part of the
other. Press lightly between two boards overnight.

Cut in fairly thick slices and arrange on a dish. Garnish
with the skin, either grilled or fried, and sprigs of dill.
*Serve with oil and vinegar, sugar, French mustard, salt
and pepper.*

The salmon could also be cut in thin slices and grilled.
Serves 6.

Fried Halibut

Halibut of about 3 lbs.
3 teaspoons salt
2 teaspoons white pepper
($\frac{1}{4}$ onion)
Vinegar

2 cups fish stock
1 teaspoon flour
1$\frac{1}{2}$ teaspoons made mustard
1 teaspoon gravy browning

Frying: 3 tablespoons butter.

Remove skin and bones and make into stock. Cut fish
in slices 2$\frac{1}{2}$ inches thick, beat lightly and put on a dish.
Sprinkle with salt, pepper and, if you like, a little finely
chopped onion. Pour over enough vinegar to barely cover
the slices. Remove them after 2 hours and wipe well.
Brown in butter and arrange on a hot dish.

Stir flour in the frying pan, add fish stock, also mustard
and gravy browning, boil for 8 minutes, season and pour
over the fish. *Serve, garnished with parsley and puff paste
crescents or squares.* Serves 6.

Fillets of Cod with Wine Sauce

2 codlings (about 1½ lbs. each)
1½ tablespoons butter
⅔ cup strong meat stock

1 small red onion
2 teaspoons salt
1½ cups fish stock
2 tablespoons white wine

Sauce:

1½ tablespoons butter
3 tablespoons flour
1½ cups of the fish stock

2 tablespoons white wine
Pinch of cayenne pepper

Cut fish into fillets but keep heads and bones. Remove skin, rinse well and wipe. Rub with salt and leave for one hour. Wipe again. Make stock from heads, bones and skin. Melt butter in fish pan, fry onion lightly, put in fillets, pour over meat stock, fish stock and wine. Boil for 10–15 minutes. Remove with fish slice to hot dish and pour over sauce. Garnish with parsley.

To make sauce, heat butter, add flour, stirring for 2 minutes, add strained fish stock gradually and boil for 8 minutes. Add wine and season with cayenne pepper.

Serve with small boiled potatoes. Serves 6.

Stuffed Haddock

1 haddock (about 4 lbs.)
1½ tablespoons salt

2 tablespoons vinegar

Stuffing:

1 cup breadcrumbs
1 cup milk
1 egg

20 anchovies
1 tablespoon chopped parsley

Coating: 1 white of egg, 1 cup breadcrumbs.

Baking-dish: 2 tablespoons butter, boiling water.

Carefully remove bone and inside by opening the back of the fish, rinse well, dry, and rub with salt and vinegar. Fillet anchovies and cut into pieces.

For the *stuffing,* mix breadcrumbs, milk, egg, anchovies and parsley. Stuff the fish and sew up along the back. Brush over with white of egg and sprinkle with breadcrumbs. Rub baking tin with butter, put in the haddock and bake in slow oven (350° F), for 20–30 minutes, basting now and again and adding boiling water at intervals. Serves 8.

Sole Au Gratin

4 soles (about 1 lb. each)	1½ teaspoons salt

Cooking:

1 tablespoon butter	2 cups fish stock

Lobster stew:

2 tablespoons butter	1 large tin lobster or
4 tablespoons flour	2 fresh lobsters
2 cups fish stock	Salt, white pepper
1 yolk	

Sauce:

2 tablespoons crayfish butter	Salt, white pepper
4 tablespoons flour	4 tablespoons grated cheese
3 cups fish stock	4 tablespoons butter

Fillet soles, but keep heads, skins and bones and make into stock. Rub fillets with salt, lay on top of each other for one hour, then cook in the stock for 5–8 minutes. Remove carefully and drain.

To make lobster stew, heat butter, add flour and cook for 2 minutes, stirring. Add fish stock gradually, stirring, and go on cooking for another 8 minutes. Add beaten yolk, while stirring briskly, *but sauce must not boil.* Mix in diced lobstermeat. Season.

Rub one or two baking or silver dishes with cold butter, arrange layers of fillets and stew, the first and last layer being fillets.

To make sauce, heat butter and crayfish butter, add flour, stirring over the fire for 2 minutes, add stock gradually, stirring, and cook for another 5 minutes. Season. Pour sauce over the fish, sprinkle with cheese, pour over 2 table-spoons melted butter and bake in moderate oven (385° F) for 15–20 minutes. *Serve with small boiled potatoes.* Serves 8.

Fried Smelts

36 smelts   Parsley (chive, dill)
1½ tablespoons salt   3 tablespoons butter

Coating: 2 eggs, 2 tablespoons breadcrumbs or coarse rye-meal.

Clean, tail and behead smelts. Remove inside and bone. Sprinkle with salt and leave for 1 hour. Chop parsley, also chive and dill, if you have any, and mix with butter. Spread out smelts flat on their backs, put two and two to-gether, sandwiched by mixture. Brush inside edges with lightly beaten eggs and press well together. Turn over in eggs, and coat with breadcrumbs and rye-meal mixed. Fry them in butter until nicely browned and *serve with Stewed Potatoes or Mashed Potatoes.* Serves 6.

Salted Herrings in Paper

2 large, or 3 smaller salted   1–2 tablespoons butter
  herrings

Fillet herrings, rinse well and leave to soak in water for 16–18 hours. Skin fillets and wipe well. Have pieces of white paper ready, butter middle part, enough to cover each fillet. Put them together two and two, wrap in paper and fry the parcels in hot dripping until paper browns. *Serve, wrapped in paper, with potatoes, boiled in their skins.* Serves 4 to 6.

Lobster Au Gratin

Boil lobsters. When cold, split in two. Remove and pound with butter the meat from the body, also claws and fins. Boil in water, skim off butter and keep for the filling.

Remove the meat from the tail and dice. Do the same with truffles, tinned mushrooms and a little blanched sweetbread. Heat lobster butter, add flour, stirring over the fire, add gradually enough thin cream to make a fairly thick stew. Cook for 10 minutes, stirring. Season with pepper, salt and a pinch of sugar. Add lobster meat, truffles, mushrooms and sweetbread. Fill shells with mixture, sprinkle with breadcrumbs and bake a light brown in moderate oven (385° F).

Swedish Fish Mould

2 cups scraped raw fish meat (hake or haddock)	1½ cups cream
	1½ cups milk
1¼ cups butter	2 teaspoons salt
4 eggs	2 teaspoons sugar
3 tablespoons flour	½ teaspoon white pepper

Fish mould (or Savarin mould):

½ tablespoon butter or crayfish butter
2 tablespoons breadcrumbs

Carefully remove all bones from the raw scraped fish. Mix with cold butter and put three times through grinder. Pound mixture in a mortar until quite smooth. Beat yolks, flour, cream and seasoning. Work into the fish in tablespoonfuls. Fold in stiffly beaten whites of egg, and add more seasoning, if necessary.

Pour into well-buttered (crayfish butter gives a nice red color) and breadcrumbed mould, about 3½ pint size. If the mould has a proper lid the fish pudding can be steamed in the ordinary way, taking 1¼ hours. Otherwise tie wax paper over the mould, place in baking tin with boiling water and cook in the oven (400° F) for one hour. Turn on to a hot dish, garnish with parsley and shrimps or mushrooms. *Serve with Mushroom Sauce or Lobster Sauce, and small boiled potatoes.* Serves 6.

Swedish Fish Soufflé

⅓ cup butter	4 eggs
½ cup flour	Salt, white pepper
2 cups milk	½ teaspoon sugar
2 cups cooked fish	

Baking-dish: ½ tablespoon butter, 2 tablespoons breadcrumbs.

Melt butter, add flour, stirring over the fire for 2 minutes. Add milk gradually, stirring well. Cook for 5 minutes, then stand aside to get cold. Add cooked, finely chopped fish and yolks. Season. Fold in gently with a knife beaten whites. Pour into buttered and breadcrumbed baking-dish. Place in tin of boiling water and bake in moderate oven (385° F) for about 30 minutes.

Serve with melted butter, or with Lobster Sauce. What is left over can be sliced and fried in butter. Serves 8.

Salted Salmon Pudding

2 cups salted salmon
1½ cups milk
3½ cups cold potatoes
3 eggs

2 teaspoons flour
¼ teaspoon white pepper
1 tablespoon fine-chopped
parsley

Baking-dish: ½ tablespoon butter, 2 tablespoons bread-crumbs.

Soak salmon overnight. Dry well and cut into slices. Slice potatoes. Fill buttered and breadcrumbed baking-dish with alternate layers of potatoes and salmon. Beat eggs with flour, add milk, beating. Season with pepper. Pour into baking-dish. Sprinkle with parsley and bake in moderate oven (385° F) for about 40 minutes. *Serve with melted butter.* Serves 8.

Kabiljo Pudding (Salt Dried Cod)

1 lb. raw salted dried cod
Or 2 cups cooked, finely-
chopped fish
1⅓ cups rice
2 cups water
3½ cups milk

2 eggs
3 tablespoons butter
½ teaspoon white pepper
Salt
1–2 teaspoons sugar

Baking-dish: ½ tablespoon butter, 3 tablespoons bread-crumbs.

Soak fish overnight. Cook, and when cold again, bone and chop finely. Clean rice, put on in cold water and, when boiling, add milk. Simmer until almost soft, add butter and leave until cold. Season, add fish and beaten eggs. Pour into buttered and breadcrumbed baking-dish, sprinkle with breadcrumbs and bake in fairly hot oven (400° F) for about an hour. *Serve with melted butter.*

Left-over pudding can be sliced and fried in butter. Serves 10.

MEAT

With the exception of veal, you get much better meat in America than in Sweden, a fact that would not strike the visitor to my country, for the simple reason that our cooks are masters in the art of disguising the slight inferiority of the raw material by clever cooking and in many cases successful camouflage, while the actual dishing up has by them been brought to a fine art.

Roasts, with the exception of loin, chicken and game are often done in large covered iron pans on top of the stove. This procedure renders the meat more tender and imparts to the gravy a richer flavor. These Swedish cast-iron stew-pans are excellent, as are also our thick iron fryingpans which are sold in the hardware departments of most leading stores.

Royal Pot Roast

3–3½ lbs. round or rump
2 tablespoons butter
½ tablespoon salt
3½ cups milk or stock
8 black peppercorns
4 white peppercorns

1 small red onion
1 bay-leaf
3 anchovies
½ tablespoon golden syrup
1 tablespoon brandy
1 tablespoon vinegar

Sauce:

½ tablespoon butter
1½ tablespoons flour

Gravy
2 tablespoons cream

Wipe meat with cloth, wrung out in hot water. Brown in hot butter in iron saucepan, add salt and boiling water, also condiments, peeled onion and anchovies, that have been tailed and beheaded, and the inside removed. Cook, covered, on the stove for about 3 hours, turning the meat a few times.

Strain and skim gravy. Heat butter, add flour, stirring over the fire. Add gravy gradually, stirring well. Cook for 10 minutes. Add cream. Serves 6.

Beef as Game

2 lbs. rump	3 tablespoons butter
$\frac{1}{4}$ lb. fat pork	1 teaspoon salt
2 cups vinegar	$\frac{1}{4}$ teaspoon white pepper
2 cups water	3 cups boiling milk

Beat meat thoroughly and lard in close rows with strips of pork. Leave overnight in vinegar and water. Dry well and tie with string to keep the shape.

Brown butter in iron saucepan, preferably just large enough to take the meat. Put in meat and brown nicely all round. Sprinkle with condiments and add boiling milk. Cook with tight lid until tender (about $2\frac{1}{2}$ hours).

Strain and skim gravy. Heat butter, add flour, stirring over the fire, add gravy gradually, stirring well. Add gravy salt or browning.

Carve the meat, arrange slices on dish, with some of the sauce poured over, garnish with fried baby potatoes, lettuce or parsley, and serve with red-currant jelly and pickled gherkins. Serves 6.

Swedish Beefsteak

2 lbs. fillet or rumpsteak	$\frac{1}{3}$ cup stock or water
2 teaspoons salt	1 large Spanish onion, or
$\frac{1}{2}$ teaspoon white pepper	3–4 red onions
4 tablespoons butter	

The meat should be well hung. Wipe with cloth wrung out in hot water. Cut across the fibres into slices, about three-quarters of an inch in thickness. Beat slices to make them thin, but do not break them. If fillet is used only tap slices with a knife-handle. Sprinkle with salt and pepper.

Peel and slice onion and fry in part of the butter. Arrange in the middle of a hot dish. Rinse frying pan in hot water, heat over brisk fire, brown enough butter to cover bottom of pan and put in meat slices. Fry 1–2 minutes on each side. Arrange round the onions. Pour over browned butter, or gravy, made by pouring some stock or water into frying pan, let it come to the boil, and strain. *Serve with fried potatoes, sprinkled with chopped parsley.* Serves 6.

Kalops

2 lbs. beef chuck or round steak	3 cups water
	1 small Spanish onion
$\frac{1}{2}$ teaspoon white pepper	3 tablespoons butter
2 teaspoons salt	12 black peppercorns
3 tablespoons flour	2 bay-leaves.

Cut meat across the fibres into slices a good $\frac{1}{2}$ inch in thickness. Remove all sinews and fat. Beat lightly.

Mix on a plate flour, white pepper and salt. Turn slices in the mixture. Peel and slice onion. Brown meat and onion quickly in the butter. Remove to saucepan. Add a

little boiling water in the frying pan and pour over the
meat. Add peppercorns, bay-leaves and the rest of the
water. Simmer with tight lid until tender. Serve in
chafing dish, with skimmed gravy poured over. Serves 6.

Sailor's Beef

2 lbs. beef chuck
2 teaspoons salt
$\frac{1}{2}$ teaspoon white pepper
1 tablespoon flour
1 large Spanish onion
3 tablespoons butter

6 medium potatoes
1$\frac{1}{8}$ cups boiling water
$\frac{1}{8}$ teaspoon meat extract
3–4 tablespoons white wine,
  sherry or beer

Prepare meat, as described above. Sprinkle with a mixture of salt, pepper and flour. Peel and slice onion and
fry in half of the butter. Peel potatoes and cut into
$\frac{1}{4}$–inch thick slices. Butter a saucepan and fill with potatoes and meat and onions in separate layers, sprinkling a
little salt on the top and bottom layers of potatoes. Pour
over water mixed with meat extract and wine. Simmer
with tight lid for about 2 hours, or until meat is tender.
If casserole is used, serve in the same. The wine might be
left out. Serves 6.

Roast Lamb

About 4 lbs. leg of lamb
2 tablespoons butter
3 tablespoons chopped
  parsley

1 carrot
2 teaspoons salt
6 black peppercorns
4 cups stock or water

Gravy: $\frac{1}{2}$ tablespoon butter, 1$\frac{1}{2}$ tablespoons flour.

Wipe meat well with cloth, wrung out in hot water.
Prick all over with skewer and stuff holes with coarsely
chopped parsley, mixed with butter. Rub baking tin with

cold butter, put meat and carrot into hot oven to brown, sprinkle with salt, pour over boiling stock or water, add peppercorns, and roast in the ordinary way, basting every 10 minutes.

Strain gravy. Heat butter, add flour, stirring, add gravy gradually, stirring well. Cook for 10 minutes.

Try basting with a cup of ordinary coffee with cream and sugar. It imparts to the gravy a rich and delicious flavor.

The carrot, baked with the lamb, improves the taste. Serves 6.

Lamb with Dill

3 lbs. shoulder of lamb	1 tablespoon salt
7 cups water	A few sprigs dill

Sauce:

1 tablespoon butter	$1\frac{1}{2}$ tablespoons vinegar
2 tablespoons flour	2 tablespoons finely-chopped dill
2 cups stock	
2 teaspoons sugar	1 yolk

Wipe meat with cloth, wrung out in hot water. Pu on in boiling water, skim when it comes to the boil again add salt and sprigs of dill. Simmer, covered, until tend , or about 2 hours. Serve, cut into pieces, with dill sauce.

To make sauce, heat butter, add flour, stirring, add stock gradually, stirring well. Cook for 8 minutes, the add vinegar, dill and last of all the yolk, after which *sau   must not boil.* Serves 6.

Larded Loin of Veal

About 5 lbs. loin of veal
$\frac{1}{3}$ lb. fat pork
2 teaspoons salt

3 tablespoons butter
1 quart stock or water

Sauce:

1 tablespoon butter
1$\frac{1}{2}$ tablespoons flour
Gravy

2 tablespoons Sherry or
  Madeira
Lemon juice
Salt, white pepper

Wipe meat with cloth, wrung out in hot water. Lard
with thin strips of fat pork, dipped in salt. Rub baking
tin with one tablespoon cold butter, put in the loin, and
pour over 2 tablespoons melted butter. Brown in fairly
hot oven (425° F), pour over boiling stock or water, and
roast in the ordinary way, basting every 10 minutes. *Time:*
about 1$\frac{1}{2}$ hours.

Skim and strain gravy. Heat butter, add flour, stirring,
add gravy gradually, stirring well, and cook for 8 minutes.
Season and add wine and lemon juice. Serves 6.

Cold Veal with Sauce Piquante

Left-over roast veal is delicious, served with Sauce
Piquante and Potato Cakes.

Veal Birds

3 lbs. fillet of veal
$\frac{1}{2}$ tablespoon salt
$\frac{1}{4}$ teaspoon white pepper
Bunch of parsley or pitted
  prunes

3$\frac{1}{2}$ tablespoons butter
4 tablespoons cream
1$\frac{1}{3}$ cups stock or water

Wipe meat with cloth, wrung out in hot water. Cut into slices across the fibres, beat lightly and sprinkle with pepper and salt. Clean parsley, chop coarsely, mix well with 2 tablespoons butter and divide into as many portions as there are slices of meat. Put one portion on each slice, roll tightly and tie securely with twine, dipped in hot water or with a toothpick. Brown "chickens" in remaining butter, add boiling stock or water and simmer, covered, in saucepan until they are tender. Remove strings and dish up.

Skim and strain gravy, add cream and pour over "chickens."

The prunes make the meat slightly sweet and very delicious. Use instead of parsley. Serves 6.

Wiener Schnitzel

2 lbs. fillet of veal	3 tablespoons butter
3 tablespoons salt	18 anchovies
1½ cups cold water	1 lemon
⅔ cup breadcrumbs	2 tablespoons capers

Wipe meat with cloth, wrung out in hot water. Cut into slices, a good ½-inch thick, and beat. Dip in salt water (3 tablespoons salt to 1½ cups water). Drain well. Turn in breadcrumbs. Heat butter in frying pan and fry schnitzels quickly on each side. Arrange on dish. Pour a little boiling water into the pan, stir well and strain over the meat.

Cut lemon into as many slices as there are schnitzels. Skin and fillet anchovies. Put two fillets in a cross on each lemon slice, sprinkle with a few capers and put one thus decorated slice on each schnitzel.

Veal Noisettes

3 lbs. loin of veal   1 cup cream
$\frac{1}{4}$ lb. pork   Salt
3 tablespoons butter   Pepper

Cut the meat in $\frac{3}{4}$-inch thick fillets and pound well on
both sides. The pork is cut in tiny strips. Make a pork
cross on each fillet and season with salt and pepper. Brown
them well in butter before pouring over the cream and
then let simmer for five minutes. Serve as dinner or
luncheon dish or on the *smörgåsbord* as a warm dish.
Serves 6.

Filet à la Oscar—I

3 lbs. fillet of veal $\frac{1}{4}$ teaspoon white pepper
1$\frac{1}{2}$ teaspoons salt   2 tablespoons butter

Sauce:

3 tablespoons crayfish   Medium tin lobster
   butter   Tin asparagus tops
2 tablespoons butter   Salt, white pepper
Asparagus liquid   Pinch of sugar
1$\frac{1}{2}$ cups thin cream

Wipe meat with cloth, wrung out in hot water. Cut into
slices, barely $\frac{1}{2}$-inch thick. Beat lightly. Sprinkle with
pepper and salt. Heat butter and fry until brown.

To make sauce, heat butter and crayfish butter, add
flour, stirring over the fire. Add asparagus liquid and
cream, stirring well. Cook for 10 minutes. Season. Add
lobster and asparagus tops, cut into pieces. Pour over
meat and serve. Serves 6.

Filet à la Oscar—II

1 lb. fillet of veal	1 teaspoon salt
2½ tablespoons butter	¼ teaspoon white pepper

Sauce:

1 teaspoon finely-chopped red onion	Cayenne pepper to taste
4 tablespoons vinegar	2 tablespoons tomato purée
3 yolks	3–4 tablespoons strong stock
Salt and pepper	
⅔ cup butter	

Garnishing: small tin asparagus tops, ½ pint shrimps, parsley.

Wipe meat with cloth, wrung out in hot water. Cut into 6 slices. Beat on both sides, and sprinkle with pepper and salt. Heat frying pan slowly. Brown the butter, and fry fillets quickly on each side.

To make the sauce, put onion, pepper, salt and vinegar in a saucepan. Reduce by boiling into a third. Place saucepan by the side of the fire and pour in beaten yolks. Stir well, *taking care not to let liquid boil.* Add gradually the butter, previously melted and cooled. Season with cayenne. Add tomato purée. Dilute with stock into creamy consistency, *being careful not to let sauce boil.*

Arrange fillets on hot dish, pour over the sauce and garnish with shrimps, asparagus and parsley. *Serve with boiled potatoes.* Serves 6.

Calf's Tongue with Madeira Sauce

1 calf's tongue	2 cups good stock
7 cups water	Gravy browning
2 teaspoons salt	1 teaspoon salt
3 tablespoons butter	White pepper

Sauce:

2 cups veal stock	2 tablespoons mushrooms,
1–2 tablespoons starch	diced and browned
1 tablespoon Madeira	

Brush tongue well, rinse and put in boiling salted water. Simmer until skin comes off easily. Brown the butter in saucepan, and brown the tongue all round. Add stock, one teaspoon salt and gravy browning, and simmer until tender, or about 40 minutes, basting every 10 minutes. Arrange in slices on hot dish and garnish with *croûtons*.

Thicken gravy with cornstarch, moistened with wine. Cook for 5 minutes, stirring well. Season and add mushrooms. Pour some of the sauce over the tongue and serve the rest separately. *Serve with fried Baby Potatoes.* Serves 6.

Loin of Pork with Prunes

3 lbs. loin of pork	$\frac{1}{2}$ tablespoon butter
$\frac{1}{2}$ lemon	2 teaspoons salt
$\frac{1}{4}$ cup prunes	2 cups stock or water
$1\frac{1}{2}$ cups water	

Wipe meat with cloth, wrung out in hot water, and rub with lemon until there is no lemon juice left. Rinse prunes, parboil (keeping liquid for the basting), stone and cut in quarters. Pierce loin with skewer in close rows and stuff holes with prunes. Rub baking tin with cold butter and put loin into hot oven to get brown, sprinkle with salt and pour over hot prune liquid. Roast in moderate oven (385° F) for about one hour, adding hot stock occasionally and basting every 10 minutes. Strain and skim gravy.

If thick sauce is wanted, heat butter, add flour, stirring, add gravy gradually, stirring, and cook for 8 minutes. Season and add a little cream. Serves 6.

Swedish Christmas Ham

Ham of 10–12 lbs.   2 tablespoons sugar
4 tablespoons salt   ½ tablespoon saltpetre

Brine:

2½ gallons water   1 oz. saltpetre
2¾ lbs. salt   ⅔ cup granulated sugar

Cooking: water (24 black peppercorns).

Coating:

½ tablespoon mustard   2 tablespoons bread-
½ tablespoon sugar   crumbs
1 egg

Rub ham with salt, sugar and saltpetre mixed. Make a
brine by boiling water with salt, saltpetre and sugar. Skim
well and leave to get cold. Put in ham and leave for
2 weeks.

Remove ham, wipe well and put on in boiling water.
When water comes to a boil again, skim, add peppercorns
and simmer for 4–5 hours. If not salt enough add more
salt during cooking.

When cooked, remove skin, brush with lightly beaten
egg, mixed with mustard and sugar. Sprinkle with breadcrumbs and leave in moderate over (400° F) for about an
hour to get a nice color.

Cover the knuckle with red and white paper frill, and
garnish with savoy cabbage, cooked prunes and cooked
mashed apples. Serves 18.

Mock Geese

12 slices lean pork   ½ teaspoon ginger
2 teaspoons salt   6 prunes
½ teaspoon white pepper   2 apples

Frying: 1 tablespoon butter, stock or water.

Beat pork slices and sprinkle with salt, pepper and ginger mixed. Put on each slice a medium-sized apple section and half a parboiled prune. Roll and tie well with twine dipped in hot water. Brown the rolls in butter in a saucepan, add stock or water, and cook, covered, for 2–2½ hours, or until tender. Turn over and baste occasionally. When done, remove string and dish up. Skin and strain gravy, season and add more water or stock, if necessary. Pour some over the "geese" and serve the rest separately. *Serve with potatoes and vegetables.* Serves 6.

Spring Chickens

3 young chickens (each about 1 lb.)	3 tablespoons butter
	2–3 teaspoons salt
Bunch of parsley	2 3 cups of water or stock

Sauce:

½ tablespoon butter	Stock
1½ tablespoons flour	6 tablespoons cream

Wipe chickens inside and outside with cloth wrung out in hot water, and dry well. Stuff birds with rinsed and dried parsley, mixed with one tablespoon butter. Sew them up and truss. Brown the rest of the butter in a saucepan, and put in the chickens, backs down. Brown them all round, add salt and boiling stock or water, and simmer, covered, until tender, basting occasionally.

To make sauce, heat butter, add flour, stirring, and gradually add skimmed and strained chicken gravy, mixed with stock, stirring well. Cook for 8 minutes. Add cream. Serves 6.

Fricassee of Chicken

2 chickens (about 6 lbs.)	1 bay-leaf, 6 white
1 lemon	peppercorns
6 cups water	1 clove
1½ tablespoons salt	Small piece of onion

Sauce:

1½ tablespoons butter	2 yolks
2 tablespoons flour	Salt, white pepper, pinch
2 cups chicken stock	of sugar
4 tablespoons cream	

Cut each chicken in 8 portions, soak well, dry, and put on in boiling water. When water comes to the boil again, skim and add onion and seasoning. Simmer gently, covered, until quite tender (1½–2 hours). Remove any pieces that are cooked before the others to a double saucepan with boiling water. Reduce stock by boiling.

For making the sauce, heat butter, add flour, stirring, and cook for 2 minutes. Add stock, gradually, stirring, and cook for 8 minutes. Season. Stir in well-beaten yolks and cream, *but the sauce must not boil afterwards.* Steep the meat in the sauce, shaking well.

Arrange boiled rice in a circle on a round dish, with the pieces of chicken forming a pyramid in the middle. Pour the sauce over, garnish with parsley, and serve very hot. Serves 6.

Chicken Fricassee with Almonds

2 small chickens or 1 large	4 cups water
1 tablespoon vinegar	1 tablespoon salt

Sauce:

1 tablespoon butter	¾ cup almonds
2 tablespoons flour	½ cup cream
4 cups stock	2 tablespoons horseradish

Wash and clean the chicken and rub it with the vinegar both inside and outside. Let it boil slowly and skim off fat.

Blanch and chop the almonds very fine and cook them in the cream with some stock. Mix butter and flour together. Add stock and cream with its almonds, season and add horseradish. Add the chicken, cut in pieces and serve with rice. Serves 6.

Roast Goose

1 young goose (about 12 lbs.)	5–6 apples
2 tablespoons salt	$\frac{1}{2}$ cup prunes
1 teaspoon white pepper	5 cups stock

A young goose should have pale red beak and feet, and the skin should be smooth, with plainly marked squares. The meat of a she-bird is more delicate than that of a gander. A goose should be hung for a few days before cooking

Wash with tepid water, brush and dry. The head, neck, wings and giblets are used for the Black Soup (See page 51). Remove the inside, rinse in cold water, dry and rub outside and inside with condiments. Stuff with peeled apple sections and parboiled prunes. Sew up, truss and put into hot oven (425° F). Baste frequently, and when a nice color, add boiling stock. Cook until tender (2–2½ hours), basting every 10 minutes. To make the skin brittle, baste only during the first hour, leaving the oven door slightly ajar afterwards.

Half an hour before the goose is ready, strain away the gravy, replacing the same with one pint boiling water. Skim gravy well, reduce by boiling, add meat extract and gravy browning, and thicken with dark thickening (See page 107).

Remove the trussing string, carve without removing the pieces, put the bird on a hot dish, garnished with baby potatoes, savoy cabbage, or parsley, and the fruit stuffing, and serve with red cabbage and pickled gherkins. Serves 12.

Grouse à la Suédois

3 grouse	2 teaspoons salt
¼ lb. fat pork, in 3 slices	1 cup stock
3 tablespoons butter	2 cups cream

The legs of a young bird are yellowish, those of older ones are reddish in color. An old bird is as good as a young one, but should be hung longer, and takes longer time roasting. Frozen ones should be kept in a warm place overnight and soaked in tepid milk for a few hours.

Tie over the breasts a slice of pork. Brown in butter in iron saucepan, together with the giblets, add salt and boiling stock, then the cream. Simmer, covered, until quite tender (about 1¼–1½ hours), basting frequently.

Young birds should not be larded. Brown in plenty of butter.

Serve with the gravy, reduced by boiling, or slightly thickened with flour.

Small birds are cut in half and served on croûtons (slices of bread, cooked in deep fat). Garnish with parsley, baby potatoes, vegetables and cooked apple halves, filled with red or black currant jelly. Also with salad. Serves 6.

Ptarmigans and Hazel-hens are treated in the same way.

Braised Wood-Grouse

1 wood-grouse	2 teaspoons salt
¼ lb. fat pork	1 cup stock
3–4 tablespoons butter	2 cups cream

The hen bird has more delicate meat than the cock, and would be enough for 6 people. A young cock is also quite good, and would be enough for 8–10 people. If frozen birds are used, leave to thaw in warm place, steep in tepid skim milk and leave to soak overnight. Wipe well, lard with thin strips of fat pork and truss. Brown in butter, in iron saucepan, add salt and boiling stock, then cream, and cook slowly, covered, until tender, or for about 2–3 hours.

To make sauce, heat butter, 1 tablespoon, add flour, 2 tablespoons for each cup of gravy, stirring, add gravy, mixed with stock or water. Stir will and cook for 8 minutes. Add cream and a lump of cold butter to make sauce smooth and glossy. If you like, flavor with one tablespoon red-currant jelly. Serves 8.

Serve with fried Baby Potatoes, mixed vegetables, red-currant jelly and Pickled Gherkins.

Braised Black Cock

2 black cocks	2 teaspoons salt
¼ lb. fat pork	1 cup stock
3–4 tablespoons butter	2 cups cream

The black hen has lighter and more delicate meat than the black cock. Proceed as described above, but the birds will only take 1½–2 hours to be done. Instead of larding, cover the breasts with thin slices of fat pork. *Serve with the same accompaniment as wood-grouse.* Serves 6.

Curried Rabbit

1 medium-size rabbit
2 teaspoons salt
3 tablespoons butter
1 red onion
3 tablespoons flour

1 teaspoon curry powder
2 cups stock
2 teaspoons lemon juice
3 tablespoons cream

Cut the rabbit into pieces. Rub with a mixture of salt and pepper. Brown butter in an iron saucepan, put in the meat, brown nicely all around and remove from pan. Fry sliced onion, flour, curry powder and butter together, add stock and let it all come to the boil. Put the meat back, add lemon juice and simmer, covered, until quite tender (about one hour). Arrange on hot dish. Pour cream into the gravy, let it come to the boil, season, if necessary, and pour over the meat.

Arrange boiled rice in a circle round the meat, and sprinkle with 1–2 teaspoons curry powder. Serves 6.

Minced Meat Dishes

Good cuts being fairly expensive in Sweden, we have learnt how to make the most of cheaper, though equally nutritious, cuts. We pin our faith to minced meat—not the coarse forbidding-looking kind you buy ready-made here in America, but the fine and wholesome stuff that can only be produced by a Swedish mincing machine. In Sweden where even the humblest meat shops are the essence of cleanliness, everything being kept behind glass and covered by glass, you can buy ready-made minced meat with confidence. But I advise my American friends to grind their meat at home. American machines grind rather coarsely, so I recommend you to get a Swedish one, which is just as cheap, and can be had from the hardware department of most leading stores. Raw beef, veal and pork make delicious mince, and my American friends have been unanimous in praising the minced meat dishes made by my Swedish cook. The main thing is to insist on the meat going through the machine three times, removing all sinews from the knife after each performance.

Swedish Meat Balls

1½ lbs. chuck meat
½ lb. fresh lean pork
2 cups water
2 or 3 eggs
½ cup breadcrumbs

1 teaspoon pepper
2 tablespoons salt
2 tablespoons chopped
    onion
butter for frying

Have meat and pork ground together. Brown onion lightly, and mix all ingredients very thoroughly with the hand until smooth and porous. Shape into small balls with a spoon, dipped in hot water. Brown evenly in butter. Remove to kettle. Make gravy by using the pan liquid and about a tablespoon of butter, two tablespoons of flour and sufficient water to make it of proper consistency. Pour over meat balls and let simmer for half an hour before serving. Half a cup of heavy cream will add to the richness and taste. Serves 6.

The meat balls can also be served dry and cold on the smörgåsbord and are delicious hors d'oeuvres at all times.

Swedish Meat Loaf

1½ lbs. chuck meat
6 oz. veal
¼ lb. fat pork
1¼ cups water
1 egg
½ cup breadcrumbs

½ teaspoon white pepper
2 teaspoons salt
2 tablespoons chopped
    onions
4 tablespoons butter

Coating: 1 egg (or white), 2 tablespoons breadcrumbs.

Baking-dish: 1½ tablespoons butter, 2 cups boiling stock or water.

Prepare meat as for meatballs. Rub a baking tin with cold butter. Put in mince and shape into a long loaf. Brush over with egg and sprinkle with breadcrumbs. Bake in moderate oven (385° F) and, when lightly browned, baste with a little boiling stock or water. Time for baking: about one hour.

The gravy could be served either plain, or as described on page 74.

Swedish meat loaf is very good served cold, with salad. Excellent for picnics. Serves 6.

Paris Snacks

White bread
2 tablespoons butter
½ lb. raw lean steak
2 tablespoons breadcrumbs
⅔ cup milk
2 teaspoons capers

1½ tablespoons chopped gherkins
2 tablespoons chopped beets
Salt, white pepper

Frying: 2 tablespoons butter.

Mince meat at least three times and mix well with breadcrumbs well soaked in milk, capers, gherkins and beets. Season. Spread slices of bread (about 3 x 2½ inches) thickly with butter. Fry on buttered side, spread fried side with thick layer of mince. Fry again, first on mince side for 1–2 minutes, then on the other side. Arrange on hot dish.

Paris Snacks can be served with a fried egg on top. In that case spread the mince on rounds of bread and trim the eggs into nice round shape, or fry them in a Swedish *Plättpanna.*

A delicious *nachspiel* dish, as a change from bacon and eggs or kippers. Serves 6.

Beef à la Lindström

1 lb. chuck steak
1½ cups milk
1 yolk
2 teaspoons salt
2 tablespoons chopped onion

3 cups cooked diced potatoes
⅔ cups diced beets
3 tablespoons pickled beet-juice
½ teaspoon white pepper
½ cup butter

Cut chuck steak into small pieces and mince at least three times. Mix well with yolk, milk, seasoning and lightly browned onions. Work well with hands. When quite smooth, mix in lightly potatoes, beets and vinegar. Shape into flat rounds, about 2½ inches across, and fry a nice color in butter. Served with fried eggs it forms a delicious *nachspiel* dish, as a change from bacon and eggs. Serves 6.

Beef à la Hazel-Hen (Beef Cutlet)

1 lb. chuck steak
⅓ lb. fat pork
1 egg
2 teaspoons salt

⅛ teaspoon white pepper
2 tablespoons potato flour
2 cups milk

Coating: 1 egg, 1 cup breadcrumbs.

Frying: 3 tablespoons butter.

Cut chuck beef, and half of the fat pork, into small pieces and mince three times. Add beaten egg, milk, potato flour and seasoning. Work well with hand. When quite smooth, shape into little cutlets. Lard with the rest of the pork, cut into thin strips. Brush with lightly beaten egg, turn in breadcrumbs and fry in butter. *Serve with peas or other vegetables.* Serves 6.

Raw Beef

4 oz. fillet of beef	2 teaspoons red onions	} finely
2 cold boiled ⎤ cut	2 teaspoons capers	⎰ chopped
potatoes ⎥ into	1 raw yolk	
1 medium-sized ⎡ tiny		
beet ⎦ dice		

Scrape meat into fine fragments with sharp knife. Shape into a flat round and chop lightly across with the back of a knife-blade, to make it look nice. Serve on small round dish, garnished with potatoes, beets, onion and capers, in separate heaps. Serve yolk in egg-cup. All ingredients to be mixed together at table. Serves 6.

Minced Veal Cutlets

1½ lb. veal	2⅓ cups milk
½ cup cooked potatoes	2 teaspoons salt
1 tablespoon chopped parsley	½ teaspoon white **pepper**

Coating: 1 egg, 2 cups breadcrumbs.

Frying: 3 tablespoons butter, 1 cup stock.

Wipe meat with cloth, wrung out in hot water. Mince three times, the last time with potatoes. Add parsley and seasoning and work mixture well with wooden spoon. When quite smooth, shape into little cutlets, brush with lightly beaten egg and coat with breadcrumbs. Heat butter in frying pan and fry cutlets a nice color. Pour over boiling stock and simmer, covered, for 5–10 minutes. *Serve with peas, spinach or mashed potatoes.* Serves 6.

Mock Ham

½ lb. smoked ham   Salt, white pepper
1 lb. lean pork   2 cups cream
5 medium-sized cooked   Red coloring matter
  potatoes

Coating: 1 egg, made mustard, breadcrumbs.

Cut ham and pork into pieces, mince five times, the last time with the potatoes. Add cream gradually, stirring well. Season and color with a little carmine. Shape on buttered baking tin into a small ham. Brush with mustard, then lightly beaten egg, and sprinkle with breadcrumbs.

Bake in fairly hot oven for 1¼–1½ hours. Pour over some stock or water, and baste often. When done, stick a skewer with a paper frill into the thin end of the "ham." Skin and strain gravy and serve separately. *Serve with green peas and carrots, and salad.* Serves 6.

Lamb with Cabbage

3 lbs. lamb (forequarter)   1½ tablespoons salt
1 head of cabbage   8 peppercorns
2 tablespoons butter   weak stock
2 tablespoons flour

Shred and parboil cabbage. Drain and brown in butter. Cut the meat in fairly large pieces and brown in fat. Place the meat and cabbage in alternate layers in a kettle with seasoning and flour in between. Cover with water or stock and let cook slowly for 3 hours. When done, skim off fat and season to taste. Serves 6.

This is a very popular Scandinavian dish.

Calf's Liver Braised Whole

2 lbs. calf's liver   ½ tablespoon sugar
¼ lb. fat pork   pepper
1 tablespoon salt

Basting: ½ quart milk or rich stock.

Gravy: 2 tablespoons flour, ¾ cup cream.

Soak the liver in milk or water for half an hour. Cut the pork in finger lengths and roll the pieces in salt and pepper. Rub the surface of the liver with the remainder of the seasoning and tie it into a neat package with a string, dipped in boiling water. Insert the lardoons by piercing the liver with a pointed knife. Sear in butter until evenly brown, add sugar, baste with milk and cook slowly in covered kettle for about 2 hours. Baste several times and turn occasionally. Remove meat from kettle, strain juice before thickening with flour and cream. Slice liver on platter and serve with the gravy poured over. Serves 6.

VEGETABLES

THE Swedish housewife always bears in mind the artistic, as well as the purely nutritious, value of vegetables. In Sweden you will find most dishes garnished with lettuce or cabbage leaves, slices of lemon, tomato or cucumber and, in some cases, radishes, beets and carrots, skilfully fashioned to represent flowers and foliage. On the *smörgåsbord* most dishes are brightened by a sprig of parsley. It is surprising what a difference just that little touch of color will make.

You will also find that, instead of serving different kinds of vegetables on separate dishes, she will arrange them in groups on one large dish, very often with the meat, already sliced, in the middle. A large silver dish, for instance, would look very nice with a cauliflower in the center, surrounded by fried baby potatoes, peas, small carrots and French beans, all in separate heaps. Fried meat could be surrounded by tomatoes, stuffed with mixed vegetables; cold meat by different salads. The idea may have originated from the necessity of facilitating the handing round, for most Swedish families, even well-to-do people, only keep one or two servants.

Lettuce with Cream

3 lettuces	$\frac{1}{3}$ teaspoon white pepper
2 hard-boiled eggs	1 teaspoon made mustard
1 raw yolk	1–2 tablespoons vinegar
1 tablespoon sugar	$\frac{2}{3}$ cup cream

Pick off decayed leaves, wash and dry lettuces, and cut the rest into large pieces. Hard-boil eggs and leave in cold water for 10 minutes to make the shells come off easily. Separate yolks and whites. When cold, mash yolks with raw yolk, salt, mustard and white pepper. Add vinegar and cream gradually, stirring well. Mix salads well with the dressing. Sprinkle with finely chopped whites. Serves 6.

Swedish Potato Salad—I

1 cup cold cooked potatoes
2 medium-sized beets
1 lettuce
2 tablespoons capers
2 yolks
½ teaspoon salt

½ teaspoon mustard
1 teaspoon sugar
1–2 tablespoons vinegar
1 tablespoon caper liquid
3 tablespoons oil
4 tablespoons cream

Slice potatoes. Cut beets into strips about an inch long. Rinse and dry lettuce and cut into long thin strips. Mix potatoes, beets, capers and lettuce in salad bowl. Stir yolks in a basin with salt, mustard and sugar. Add oil, vinegar and caper liquid gradually, stirring. Add cream, stirring, and pour sauce over salad, mixing well. Serves 6.

Swedish Potato Salad—II

About 1 lb. small potatoes
1 tablespoon butter
2 tablespoons flour
⅔ cup cream
2 tablespoons vinegar
½ teaspoon salt

1 teaspoon sugar
Tiny pinch cayenne pepper
1–2 tablespoons capers
½ tablespoon finely chopped chives

Boil potatoes in their skins in slightly salted water. Skin and, when cold, cut into thin even slices and arrange in salad bowl.

Heat butter, add flour, stirring over the fire, add cream gradually, stirring well. Cook for 10 minutes. Season and add vinegar. Pour dressing over potatoes, mixing gently. When cold, garnish with capers and chives. Serves 6.

Stuffed Tomatoes

6 large firm tomatoes
½ cup cold veal
½ cup tongue
½ cup salt or smoked beef

1 cup cooked carrots
1 small pickled gherkin
2 apples
1 cup French beans

Mayonnaise:

2 yolks
½ teaspoon salt
Pinch cayenne
¼ teaspoon French
  mustard
6 tablespoons olive oil

1 tablespoon Tarragon
  vinegar
½ tablespoon lemon juice
1 tablespoon boiling
  water

Garnishing: 2 tablespoons finely chopped truffles.

Cut veal, tongue, salt beef, carrots, gherkin and apples into tiny dice. Cut beans into tiny square pieces. Mix well with mayonnaise.

To make mayonnaise, mix well yolks, pepper, salt and mustard with wooden spoon. Add vinegar gradually, stirring vigorously. Add oil, first drop by drop, then more quickly, stirring evenly. Last of all add lemon juice and boiling water to prevent mayonnaise from curdling. Leave for a few hours in a cool, but not too cold, place to thicken.

Should the mayonnaise curdle in the making, stir in a yolk and ½ tablespoon vinegar.

Scoop out tomatoes, fill with salad and sprinkle with truffles. *Serve with cold beef or ham, or as an entrée.* Serves 6.

Fried Baby Potatoes

2 lbs. potatoes	2 tablespoons butter
Water	3 tablespoons breadcrumbs
2 teaspoons salt	2 teaspoons sugar

Boil potatoes in their skins. When cold, peel and cut into small balls. (The cuttings can be used for potato cakes.) Shake potato balls in a mixture of breadcrumbs, salt and sugar. Brown butter in frying pan, put in potatoes and sprinkle with breadcrumbs that have not adhered to them. Fry a nice color, shaking the pan. *Serve with roasted meat, chicken and game.* Serves 6.

Fried Potatoes

1½ lbs. cooked potatoes	1 teaspoon sugar
2½ tablespoons butter	1 tablespoon finely
2 tablespoons breadcrumbs	chopped parsley
1 teaspoon salt	

Peel potatoes and cut into fairly thin slices or cubes. Brown half of the butter in frying pan, put in potatoes and sprinkle with mixture of breadcrumbs, salt and sugar. Put the rest of the butter on top and fry a nice color, shaking the pan continuously. Sprinkle with parsley. *Serve with fried fish or meat.* Serves 6.

Mashed Potatoes

4 lbs. potatoes
Water, salt
2 cups milk

2 tablespoons butter
1 teaspoon sugar
1 teaspoon salt

Peel and cook potatoes. Mash well with a fork. Add boiling milk. Stir in cold butter, add sugar and salt. Beat into a light froth. Serves 6.

Potato Cakes

1½ lbs. cooked potatoes
1 tablespoon butter
1 yolk
1–2 tablespoons cream

1 teaspoon salt
1 teaspoon sugar
(Dash of nutmeg)

Coating and Frying: 4 tablespoons breadcrumbs, 2 tablespoons butter.

Mash potatoes well. Stir butter until creamy and mix well with potatoes, yolk, cream and seasoning. Shape into balls with two spoons, dipped in flour. Flatten balls, turn in breadcrumbs and fry a nice color in butter. *Serve with fried fish or meat.* Serves 6.

Potato Éclairs

½ cup butter
2 cups water
2 cups flour

4 eggs
2 cups mashed potatoes
Salt, pinch of sugar

Cooking: 4 cups lard.

Boil butter and water and, while still boiling, add flour, beating well. Cook until mixture turns a yellow tint and comes away from the sides of the saucepan. Allow to cool.

Beat in eggs, one at a time, and stir for 10 minutes. Add cold mashed potatoes, stirring vigorously. Season.

Have ready boiling deep fat, dip two spoons in flour and shape mixture into little balls, cook a golden brown in the fat and drain on kitchen paper. *Serve with fried or roast meat.*

The éclairs could be filled with peas or chopped truffles. If plain, make them quite small. Serves 6.

Potatoes Au Gratin

1 lb. peeled raw potatoes	1 egg
1 teaspoon salt	2 cups boiling milk
¼ teaspoon white pepper	⅓ cup grated fresh
(Dash of grated nutmeg.)	gruyère cheese

Omelette dish: 1 slice onion, 3 tablespoons butter, 2 tablespoons grated gruyère cheese.

Peel potatoes, rinse and dry, and cut into thin slices. Mix well with beaten egg, boiled milk, seasoning and cheese.

Rub omelette dish with onion slice, then with half of butter. Arrange potato slices, sprinkle with cheese and dot with the rest of the butter. Bake in hot oven (400° F) until potatoes are soft, or for about 45 minutes. *Serve with the hors d'oeuvres, or with fried and boiled sausages.* Serves 6.

Stewed Potatoes

1½ lbs. cooked potatoes	Salt
1½ tablespoons butter	2 tablespoons chopped
1½ tablespoons flour	parsley
1 cup milk	

Boil potatoes in their skins. When cold, peel and cut into thin slices. Heat butter, add flour, stirring over the fire, add milk gradually, stirring until the consistency of fairly thick white sauce is obtained. Cook for 2 minutes. Add potato slices and cook for another 5 minutes. Season, and stir in finely chopped parsley. *Serve with fried sausage, or salted salmon.* Serves 6.

Swedish Spinach

1½ lb. spinach	½ tablespoon sugar
3 tablespoons flour	1½ cups stock, milk or
2 tablespoons butter	water
	1½ teaspoons salt

Garnishing: 1 hard-boiled egg.

Clean spinach, rinse quickly and drain. Put on in very little boiling salted water and cook for a few minutes. Drain. Chop finely together with flour. Heat butter in a saucepan, put in spinach and add gradually stock, milk or water, stirring well. Cook for 10 minutes. Season. Dish up and sprinkle with hard-boiled egg, white and yolk chopped separately.

Served with fried fish or meat; also with smoked salmon. Serves 6.

Glazed Carrots

12 small carrots	2 tablespoons butter
Water	2 teaspoons sugar
Salt	

Rinse carrots and boil in salted water until tender. Drain and peel while still hot. Melt butter and sugar in a saucepan, put in carrots and leave until well covered with glaze. *Serve with roast meat.*

Carrot Pudding

1½ lbs. carrots	2 eggs
6 tablespoons soft	1 cup milk
breadcrumbs	1 teaspoon salt
2 tablespoons butter	

Baking-dish: ½ tablespoon butter, 2 tablespoons bread-crumbs.

Parboil and grate carrots. Beat eggs, add milk, butter, breadcrumbs and salt, and mix with carrots. Pour into buttered and bread-crumbed baking-dish and bake in moderate oven (385° F). *Serve with fish or meat.* Serves 6.

Mashed Turnips

1 large turnip	4 tablespoons cream
2 cups weak stock	2 teaspoons salt
1½ lbs. potatoes	2 teaspoons sugar
2 tablespoons butter	¼ teaspoon white pepper

Peel and cube turnip. Put on in stock and parboil (about 15 minutes). Peel and cube potatoes. Add to turnip and boil until tender. Pour off superfluous liquid, and mash potatoes and turnip with a fork. Add cold butter and cream, beating well. Season. *Serve with salt or smoked beef, pork or sausage.* Serves 6.

Swedish Turnips

2 large turnips	2 tablespoons brown sugar
5 cups water ⎱ for	1 teaspoon salt
2 teaspoons salt ⎰ cooking	1½ cups thin stock
4 tablespoons butter	¼ teaspoon white pepper

Peel turnips and cut into ½-inch cubes. Put on in boiling salted water and, when it comes to the boil again, cook until thoroughly parboiled (½ hour).

Brown butter in a saucepan, add turnips, sprinkle with sugar and salt and keep on stirring until they are nicely browned. Add stock, and simmer until tender, or about 1½ hours. Season with a little pepper. *Serve with salt beef and as garnish around a platter of mashed potatoes.* Serves 6.

Stewed White Cabbage

1 medium-size white cabbage
Water

Vinegar
Salt

White sauce:

2 tablespoons butter
4 tablespoons flour

3 cups cabbage liquid or milk
Salt, sugar

Pick off discolored leaves, remove stalk and divide cabbage into 6–8 pieces. Soak for ⅛ hour in water and vinegar (one tablespoonful vinegar to every quart water). Put on in boiling salted water and cook for 10 minutes. Remove to another saucepan with boiling water and simmer until quite tender. Heat butter in a saucepan, add flour, stirring over the fire. Add cabbage liquid, or milk, gradually, stirring. Cook for 10 minutes. Season. Dish up cabbage and pour sauce over.

Serve with fried meat, sausage, and minced meat dishes. Serves 6.

Swedish Brown Beans

2 cups brown beans
5 cups water

3–4 tablespoons golden syrup
3–4 tablespoons vinegar

Brown beans are very nourishing and a favorite food in Sweden. They can be bought from most big stores.

Rinse beans and put on in cold water. Simmer until tender (about 3 hours), adding hot water occasionally, if necessary. When cooked, add syrup, vinegar to taste, and a pinch of salt.

Serve with fried bacon or pork, Swedish Meat Balls or Meat Loaf.

The beans will take shorter time to cook if soaked overnight, but it will turn them greyish. Serves 6.

SAUCES

THAT "it is the sauce that lends character to a dish" seems to be the ruling maxim of every Swedish cook, and one that she shares with her French colleagues. We know that the French Marquis de la Revelière once received Le Cordon Bleu, the highest official recognition for culinary ability, as a reward for inventing a marvellous sauce which contained 27 different ingredients and which took him 11 hours to make. The sauces, described in this book, only take about 10 minutes, and they are well worth the trouble. But you should bear the following hints in mind.

Only use best butter and flour, being careful to have the right quantity to make the sauce nice and smooth.

Most thick sauces are made by heating butter, next adding flour, stirring over the fire for 2 minutes. Then liquid gradually, stirring well, and cooking for 5–10 minutes.

When using eggs to thicken a sauce, beat before adding the same, with 2 tablespoonfuls of the liquid, add to the sauce, and heat until it thickens, *but do not let it boil*, stirring well all the time. A lump of butter, added last of all, improves a sauce of this description. Be sparing with seasoning and essences. A well-made sauce should be smooth and glossy and have a decided, clean taste without unnecessary additions.

To make a sauce darker and stronger in flavor, mix flour and butter, leave by the side of the fire, stirring now and again until the mixture turns a light brown. Then proceed as described above.

When thickening with potato flour, or cornflour, dilute first with a little cold water. Move saucepan to the side of the fire and, when the boiling has subsided, add thickening agency. Boil, stirring, for 5 minutes. Potato flour only takes 2 minutes.

Gravy

GRAVY is made by adding boiling water to the sediment which remains in the baking tin or frying pan after the fat has been skimmed off. When there is not sufficient gravy, meat extract may be used. The best gravy stock, however, is made like this:

Cut into pieces some gravy beef (neck or leg), and raw or cooked remains of veal, mutton, pork or chicken or game, bones and sinews. Brown plenty of butter or dripping in an iron stewpan, put in meat and bones and brown well, together with a couple of peeled sliced onions, 2 carrots and one celery root, scraped and sliced. Also a few white peppercorns. When meat is browned, only just cover with weak stock or water. Skim well and simmer for 5–6 hours. Strain through hair sieve or cloth. Simmer a little longer if you like. Leave until following day, to allow the fat to rise to the top. Do not remove the fat until you wish to use the gravy. If you only use part of the gravy, boil again with the fat and leave to set. Treated in this way the gravy will keep for several weeks.

After roasting and frying meat, strain gravy, pour some boiling stock in the pan and strain with the rest of the gravy. Leave for 5–10 minutes to allow the fat to rise to the top, skim well and proceed as already described. The gravy should not be thickened for sirloin.

Fine Fishsauce

¾ cups butter
4 yolks

1½ cups cream
Lemon juice

Melt the butter in top of double boiler. Have water underneath simmering, not boiling. Beat the yolks with cream until stiff. Add cream and eggs and beat constantly. Continue until the sauce is foamy and slightly thick. Then remove from stove and add lemon juice to taste. Delicious with all fish, as well as boiled artichokes and broccoli served as separate dishes.

Special Sauce

(For boiled tongue or ham)

3 cups of stock
1 tablespoon vinegar
1 tablespoon sugar
¼ cup currants

¼ cup blanched, chopped
    almonds
10 gingersnaps for
    thickening

Mix all the ingredients together and let it simmer for a few minutes. Slice the tongue or ham and place it in a kettle with the sauce over it to draw a while before serving. This sauce makes a festive dish of any common food.

Gravy for Roasts

1 tablespoon butter
2 tablespoons flour
2 cups gravy

(4 tablespoons cream)
Salt
White pepper

Heat butter, add flour, stirring over the fire, add gravy gradually, stirring, and cook for 10 minutes. Cream should be added now. It gives a nice rich flavor, but is not necessary. Season. A teaspoonful of cold butter, stirred in last of all, improves the gravy.

Brown Mushroom Sauce

Small bottle mushrooms or 2 cups gravy
  ¼ lb. fresh mushrooms   2 tablespoons mushroom
1½ tablespoons butter   liquid
2 tablespoons flour   Salt, white pepper

Cut mushrooms into slices, or cubes, and brown in butter until it is quite clear. Press mushrooms away from the saucepan with a spoon, leaving the butter. Add flour to butter and cook for 2 minutes, stirring. Add gravy and mushroom liquid gradually, stirring, and cook for 10 minutes. Add mushrooms and season. A little Madeira or white wine might be added.

Serve with red meat dishes or fish (made with fish stock).

Horseradish Sauce

1 tablespoon butter   3–4 tablespoons grated
2 tablespoons flour   horseradish
1½ cups stock or milk   Salt, pinch of sugar

Scrape horseradish, rinse and keep in cold water for an hour. Dry and grate. Heat butter, add flour, stirring for 2 minutes, over the fire, add stock or milk gradually, stirring. Cook for 8 minutes. Add horseradish and season, *but do not let the sauce boil afterwards,* as it gets a bitter taste. A lump of cold butter, added last of all, improves the sauce.

Serve with boiled meat or fish.

Dill Sauce

1 tablespoon butter   2 teaspoons sugar
2 tablespoons flour   1½ tablespoons vinegar
1½ cups stock   Salt
2 tablespoons chopped dill 1 yolk

Heat butter, add flour, stirring for 2 minutes over the fire. Add stock gradually, stirring. Cook for 8 minutes. Add vinegar and dill, and season. Stir in beaten yolk, but *the sauce must not boil afterwards.*

Serve with Boiled Lamb or Veal.

Bottled dill can be bought in the grocery department of most leading stores.

Mock Hollandaise Sauce

4 tablespoons butter
1 tablespoon flour
Salt, white pepper, sugar

4 yolks
⅔ cup water
1 teaspoon lemon juice

Stir butter in a warmed saucepan until it melts. Stir in flour and cook until it bubbles. Remove from fire and add yolks, one at a time, salt, pepper and sugar to taste. Place saucepan over very slow fire, add cold water gradually, stirring well, and let the sauce get hot, but *it must not boil.* When thick and glossy, remove from fire and add lemon juice. Place saucepan in boiling water until ready to serve.

Serve with fish.

Lemon Sauce

3½ tablespoons butter
2 cups cream
Salt, sugar to taste
½ small lemon

2 tablespoons finely
  chopped parsley
3 yolks

Melt butter, add well-beaten yolks, cream and seasoning, stirring well over very slow fire, until sauce is thick, but *it must not boil.* Add grated lemon peel and lemon juice, also more seasoning, if necessary. Last of all add parsley,

steeped for a few minutes in slightly salted boiling water. Keep saucepan in hot water until ready to serve.
Serve with fish.

Wine Sauce

3 tablespoons butter
4 tablespoons flour
2 cups good fish stock

1–2 yolks
Salt, white pepper
2 tablespoons white wine

Heat butter, add flour, stirring over the fire for 2 minutes. Add fish stock gradually, stirring, and cook for 8 minutes. Add well-beaten yolks, whisking but be very careful not to let the sauce boil. Season and add wine.
Serve hot with fish.

Butter Sauce

1½ tablespoons butter
3 tablespoons flour
1½ cups slightly salted
  boiling water
3 yolks

4 tablespoons cream
1 teaspoon lemon juice
5 tablespoons butter,
  melted

Stir butter and flour over the fire for 2 minutes, being careful not to let it get brown. Add boiling salted water gradually, and boil. Beat cream and yolks well together and add, but *sauce must not boil.* Add lemon juice to taste. Pass through straining cloth and stir in melted butter.
Serve with fish, meat or vegetables.

Lobster Sauce

1 tablespoon butter
1 teaspoon crayfish butter
3 tablespoons flour
1 cup fish stock
2 cups cream

1 medium tin lobster (or a medium-sized fresh lobster)
Salt, white pepper, sugar
1–2 yolks

Heat butter and crayfish butter, add flour, stirring over the fire for 2 minutes. Add fish stock and cream gradually, stirring, and cook for 5 minutes. Add well-beaten yolks and diced lobster, also liquid from the tin. Season. *The sauce must not boil after the yolks have been added.*

Serve with boiled fish.

Crayfish butter can be had from most leading stores.

Mustard Sauce

2 tablespoons butter
3 tablespoons flour
2–3 teaspoons mustard powder

2 cups fish stock
Salt, sugar to taste
(1 yolk)
½ tablespoon cold butter

Heat butter, add flour and mustard powder, stirring over the fire for 2 minutes, add fish stock gradually, stirring, and cook for 8 minutes. Season. A pinch of sugar improves the taste. A well-beaten yolk might be added, but is not necessary. Stir in cold butter. A finely chopped hard-boiled egg might be stirred in last of all.

Serve with boiled fish or as a separate dish on the *smörgåsbord* with hard-boiled eggs, halved.

Caper Sauce

1½ tablespoons butter
3 tablespoons flour
2 cups fish stock or
   ordinary stock
4 tablespoons cream
1–2 tablespoons caper
   liquid

Salt, white pepper, sugar
2 tablespoons chopped
   capers
1–2 yolks
½ tablespoon cold butter
   (not necessary)

Heat 1½ tablespoons butter, add flour, stirring over the fire for 2 minutes. Add stock and cream, gradually, stirring, and cook for 8 minutes. Add capers and caper liquid, and let sauce come to the boil. Season. Stir in well-beaten yolk, and cold butter.

Serve with fish or with boiled shoulder of lamb or veal.

Cooked Mayonnaise

1½ tablespoons butter
4 tablespoons flour
½ tablespoon mustard
⅓ teaspoon white pepper
1½ cups stock

1 tablespoon sugar
3 yolks
2 tablespoons olive oil
3 tablespoons vinegar
1 cup cream

Heat butter, flour, mustard and white pepper, stirring over the fire for 2 minutes. Add fish—or meat—stock gradually, stirring, and cook into consistency of a thick gruel. Pass through fine sieve and stir until cold. Add sugar and yolks, one at a time, stirring. Also oil and vinegar, first drop by drop, then more quickly, stirring steadily. Add whipped cream last of all.

Serve with cold salmon, or other cold fish.

Sauce Piquante

2 hard-boiled yolks
1 raw yolk
1 tablespoon sugar
⅓ teaspoon white pepper

Pinch of salt
About 1 teaspoon mustard
1–1½ tablespoons vinegar
1 cup cream

Rub yolks, sugar, pepper, salt, mustard and vinegar well with wooden spoon. Add whipped cream gradually.
Serve with cold fish or with cold veal.

Cream Dressing

1 cup cream
2 yolks
1 teaspoon mustard

1½ tablespoons vinegar
1½ tablespoons sugar
Pinch of white pepper

Whip cream to a froth, stir in yolks, one at a time, add vinegar. Season.
Serve with fish aspics.

Herring Salad Dressing

1½ cups cream
¼ teaspoon salt
¼ teaspoon white pepper

2–3 teaspoons sugar
2–3 tablespoons beet
  liquid

Whip cream to a froth, add beet liquid and seasoning.
Serve with Herring Salad.

Iced Horseradish Sauce

2 cups cream
4 tablespoons vinegar
3–4 tablespoons sugar

7–8 tablespoons grated
  horseradish
(Pinch of white pepper)
Ice, coarse salt

Scrape, rinse and grate horseradish a little while before using, but keep covered. Beat cream to a froth, add vine-

gar and horseradish, and season.   Serve very cold, preferably iced.   When ready, scoop out with spoon, dipped in
hot water, and serve in cooled sauce tureen.

Serve with duck, wild duck or goose.

Creamed Butter

1 cup butter $\frac{1}{2}$–1 teaspoon lemon juice
Pinch of salt

Stir butter with wooden spoon in a basin, kept over hot
water.   When white and creamy, add lemon juice.   Put
into sauce boat with a teaspoon, dipped in hot water.

Serve with asparagus, artichokes and other vegetables.

SWEET SAUCES

Plain Vanilla Sauce

½ teaspoon vanilla extract
1 cup milk
1 cup cream

1–2 tablespoons sugar
¼ tablespoon potato flour
3 yolks

Bring to a boil milk, cream and sugar. Add potato flour, mixed with a little cold milk. Boil for 2 minutes. Place saucepan by the side of the fire and add yolks. Beat briskly over slow fire until sauce thickens, but *it must not boil.* Keep on beating until cold. Add vanilla and mix. *Serve with stewed fruit and fruit pies.*

Foundation for Sweet Sauces

2 yolks
2 tablespoons sugar

½ tablespoon potato flour
1 cup milk

Cream yolks and sugar. Add potato flour, mixed with one tablespoon cold milk. Boil the rest of the milk and stir briskly into mixture. Stir over slow fire until sauce thickens, but *it must not boil.* Keep on beating until cold. Flavor with *rum, arrack, fruit, syrup, lemon, orange, vanilla, caramel, coffee or chocolate.*

Serve hot or cold. To keep hot, place saucepan in another one with boiling water.

117

Plain Lemon Sauce

1 lemon (grated peel and juice)
4 tablespoons white wine
1 cup water
4 tablespoons sugar
2 teaspoons potato flour
2 yolks

Grate off yellow part from lemon peel and press out the juice. Put all ingredients into saucepan and stir vigorously over the fire until sauce thickens, but *it must not boil.* Remove from fire and keep on stirring until cold. *Serve with sweet puddings or fruit pies.*

Lemon Sauce with Cream

1 lemon
2 tablespoons white wine
2 tablespoons water
2½ tablespoons sugar
3 yolks
About 2 cups cream

Grate off yellow parts from lemon peel and press out the juice. Put into saucepan with wine, water, sugar and yolks, and stir vigorously over very low fire until sauce thickens, but *it must not boil.* Remove from fire and keep on stirring until cold. Add cream, whipped to a stiff froth.

Wine Sauce

6 yolks
3 tablespoons sugar
1½ cups white wine
½ lemon (grated peel and juice)

Grate off yellow part from lemon peel and press out the juice. Put all ingredients into a saucepan and beat vigorously over slow fire until sauce has risen to twice its original volume, but *it must not boil.* Remove from fire and *serve at once.*

Orange Sauce

3 yolks
2 whites of eggs
¾ cup sugar

1 lemon
2 oranges
1½ cups cream

Stir yolks with half of the sugar for 20 minutes. Beat white to a stiff froth and mix with the rest of the sugar. Stir both mixtures well together and mix with the juice of 2 oranges and grated peel and juice of a lemon. Last of all fold in whipped cream and *serve at once.*

Fruit Syrup Sauce

1 cup sweet fruit syrup
1 cup water

2 tablespoons potato flour
Lemon juice

Let water and fruit syrup come to the boil. Mix potato flour with a little cold water, add and boil for 2 minutes. Sweeten, if necessary, and add lemon juice to taste. *Serve hot or cold with sweet puddings made with rice or flour.*

Chocolate Sauce

2 cups water
¾ cup cocoa
3 teaspoons potato flour

Sugar to taste
1 cup cream

Boil water, add cocoa, stirring well, then potato flour, mixed with a little cold water. Boil for 2 minutes. Add sugar to taste and mix with whipped cream. *Serve cold.*

PUDDINGS AND SWEETS

Anna's Apple Pudding

6 medium apples
1 tablespoon sugar
1 cup butter

1 cup brown sugar
2 cups flour

Prepare apples in baking-dish as for deep-dish apple pie, with the sugar over it. Make crust of butter, brown sugar and flour and cover the dish. Bake in moderate oven (385° F) until apples are cooked and the crust is a taffy brown. *Serve hot with whipped cream.* Serves 6.

Apples à la Finesse

15 big apples
3 tablespoons butter
1 cup coarse sugar

1 cup breadcrumbs
1 cup chopped nuts or
   almonds

Peel and core the apples. Mix breadcrumbs, nuts and sugar (granulated will do!). Melt the butter. Roll the apples first in butter and then in the nut mixture and bake to a light brown. *Serve cold with whipped cream or vanilla sauce.* Serves 12.

Dutch Rice Pudding

$\frac{3}{4}$ cup rice
$3\frac{1}{2}$ cups milk
1 teaspoon vanilla
1 cup thick cream

3 tablespoons sugar
$1\frac{1}{4}$ teaspoons gelatine
2 tablespoons cold water

120

Cook the rice in milk and chill. Add sugar, vanilla and gelatine which was first soaked in cold water and dissolved over the flame. Fold in beaten cream and chill in mould several hours before unmoulding. *Serve with fruit sauce.* Serves 6.

Crisp Pancakes

1½ cups water
1⅓ cups flour

⅔ cup butter
1½ cups cream

Stir water and sifted flour well together, and leave for 2 hours. Melt butter and, when cooled, add to the batter, together with sugar and hard-whipped cream. Heat pancake pan slowly, brush with butter only for the first pancake. Make thin pancakes, only frying them on one side. When a light brown, roll them up with a fork. *Serve hot with jam.* Serves 6.

Swedish pancake pans (plättlagg) are excellent for pancakes and tarts and can be used also for making small cakes and for frying eggs. They are quite inexpensive and can be had from the hardware department of most leading stores.

Plättar (Small Pancakes)

2 eggs
3 cups milk
3 teaspoons sugar

1⅓ cups flour
1 teaspoon salt

Frying: 2 tablespoons butter.

Beat eggs and add milk and flour gradually with salt and sugar. Heat pancake pan slowly, brush with melted butter. Stir batter well and bake thin and light pancakes. *Serve hot with jam.* Serves 6.

Pancakes with Meringue or Cream

3 yolks
1 cup cream
1⅓ cup flour

3 cups milk
¼ teaspoon salt
1½ tablespoons butter

Frying: 2 tablespoons butter.

Filling and garnishing: Raspberry or strawberry jam, 3 whites of egg, 1 cup powdered sugar (or ½ pint cream and ½ tablespoon powdered sugar), ¼ cup almonds.

Beat yolks, add cream, and then stir in sifted flour. Add milk gradually, also salt and melted butter. Leave for 2 hours. Heat pancake pan slowly, and brush with melted butter. Stir batter well and bake *thin* pancakes. Pile them on hot dish, spreading each pancake thinly with jam, warmed in double saucepan. Cut pancake pile in 12 sections and leave to get cold.

Beat whites stiffly. Sift sugar gently into whites, spread over pancakes and sprinkle with scalded finely chopped almonds. Put into cool oven (325° F) and leave until partly set and just turning a golden color.

The pancakes could also be spread with sweetened hard whipped cream, and sprinkled with chopped almonds. Serves 8.

Crisp Waffles

1 pint cream (sweet or sour)
1⅓ cups flour

½ cup butter
4 tablespoons cold water or 1 cup fine snow

Waffle iron: ½ tablespoon butter.

Whip cream to a stiff froth, add flour and water, and let cool for about an hour. Stir in melted butter gently. To make waffles crisp and a good color the heat must be kept even. Heat waffle iron slowly on both sides, brush with melted butter, and pour into it a ladleful of batter. Turn iron, and be sure always to have the hottest side on top while the waffles are being baked. Remove waffles with a fork, trim with scissors, and put on a cake cooler to keep them crisp. Pile on hot dish, and *serve with jam or compôte.*

Swedish waffle iron, making five heart-shaped waffles, can be had from the hardware department of most leading stores. They are quite inexpensive and easy to use.

Cream Waffles

1 egg
6 tablespoons water
3 tablespoons butter

1½ cups flour
½ pint cream

Waffle iron: ½ tablespoon butter.

Beat egg and water into a froth. Add melted butter, flour and stiffly whipped cream. *Proceed, as described above.* Serves 4.

Poor Knights (French Toast)

2 eggs
3 cups milk
4 tablespoons flour

2 teaspoons sugar
18 slices from stale loaf
of bread

Frying: 4 tablespoons butter.

Beat eggs, add some of the milk and sugar, add flour and more milk, keeping ¾ pint. Dip slices of bread first in milk and then in batter. Fry a nice golden brown in butter. *Serve with jam.* Serves 6.

Rich Knights (Cream French Toast)

24 thin slices of stale bread
$\frac{1}{3}$ cup ground almonds
$\frac{1}{3}$ cup powdered sugar
$\frac{1}{2}$–1 tablespoon water

$\frac{2}{3}$ cup mashed cooked apples
2 cups cream
$\frac{2}{3}$ cup breadcrumbs
4 tablespoons butter

Pound almonds, sugar and water into a smooth consistency. Spread on one bread slice, spreading another with mashed apples. Put slices together, dip in cream, turn in breadcrumbs and fry a nice golden brown in butter. *Serve hot with sugar.* Serves 8.

Swedish Rice Pudding

$\frac{2}{3}$ cup rice
3 tablespoons butter
5 cups milk
$\frac{1}{2}$ teaspoon salt

2–3 tablespoons sugar
8 bitter almonds
$\frac{1}{3}$ cup raisins
2–3 eggs

Baking-dish: $\frac{1}{2}$ tablespoon butter, 2 tablespoons breadcrumbs.

Rinse rice in cold water, put on in boiling slightly salted water and boil briskly for 15 minutes. Draw and rinse under cold water and drain. Put into saucepan, divide butter into small portions and stir into rice with a fork. Cover saucepan and leave in hot oven (400° F) for about 15 minutes, stirring often with a fork. Pour into mixing bowl and mix with cold butter, salt, sugar blanched and grated almonds and well-rinsed and scalded seedless raisins. When cold, stir in well-beaten yolks. Pour into buttered and bread-crumbed baking-dish, and bake in moderate oven (385° F) for 40–50 minutes. *Serve only just warm, with jam, compôte or Fruit Syrup Sauce.* Serves 6.

Swedish Christmas Porridge

In Sweden Christmas Eve is the principal day of celebration, and supper that night consists of *"Lutfisk,"* fish that has been steeped in lye, and *"Julgröt,"* or Christmas Porridge. An almond is hidden in the porridge, and the person who finds the almond will be the first one to get married. Here is the recipe for the porridge:

1 cup rice	½ pint cream
4 cups water	1 teaspoon salt
½ cup butter	1 tablespoon sugar

Rinse and scald rice, put on in boiling water and cook slowly until soft (about one hour). Add cold butter and hard whipped cream. Heat porridge, but *do not let it boil.* Add salt and sugar. *Serve with cold milk.* Serves 6.

Stuffed Apples

12 medium-sized apples	1 cup breadcrumbs
4 tablespoons melted butter	2 tablespoons sugar

Baking tin: 1 tablespoon butter.

Almond paste:

⅔ cup ground almonds	1 white of egg
½ cup powdered sugar	

Pound almonds and sugar well together. Mix with stiffly beaten white. Peel and core apples. Fill with almond paste. Dip into melted butter and turn in sugar and breadcrumbs mixed. Put into buttered tin, pour over the rest of the butter and bake to a nice color in moderate oven (385° F).

Serve with Vanilla Sauce, or ordinary custard, with a little vanilla essence added, and mixed with whipped cream. Serves 6.

Swedish Apple Pudding

2½ lbs. fresh apples
⅔ cup sugar
½ cup water

½ stale brown loaf (about 2 cups breadcrumbs)
½ cup butter

Peel apples, core and cut into thin sections. Cook into pulp with sugar and very little water. Grate the loaf (or pass through a mincer), and brown lightly in ½ cup of butter. Spread buttered and breadcrumbed tin with three layers of breadcrumbs and two of apples, the top layer of breadcrumbs. Dot on top with the rest of the butter. Bake for ½ hour in moderate oven (385° F). Turn out and sprinkle with sugar. *Serve hot or cold, with whipped cream or Vanilla Sauce.*

A can of any good applesauce will serve the purpose very nicely. Serves 6.

Rhubarb Pie

1¼ cups flour
⅞ cup butter
½ cup sugar

1 egg
5 bitter almonds
10 almonds

Filling: 1¼ lb. rhubarb, 1¼ cups sugar.

Cake-tin: ½ tablespoon butter, 2 tablespoons breadcrumbs.

Wash butter and work into it sugar, flour, ground almonds and egg. When quite smooth, leave in cold place for 2 hours.

Trim rhubarb, and cut into lengths of about 2 inches. Roll out two-thirds of the short paste and line a buttered cake tin, or Swedish cast iron frying pan, arrange layers of rhubarb, each layer sprinkled with sugar, and fold over the edges of the short paste. Roll out the rest of the paste and cover pie, pressing edge together. Bake for an hour in fairly cool oven (350° F). Test with a match whether the crust is baked through. Remove from oven and leave for 15 minutes before turning out. *Serve hot or cold, with whipped cream or Vanilla Sauce, or plain custard, with a little vanilla essence added, and mixed with some whipped cream.*

Apples or gooseberries might be used instead of the rhubarb. Serves 6.

Fruit Syrup Cream

2⅝ cups sweet fruit syrup   4–5 tablespoons potato
4 cups water   flour
Lemon juice

Mix fruit syrup and water, boil, and add sugar, if necessary. Stir potato flour with a little cold water, add to liquid and boil for 2 minutes, stirring. Add lemon juice. Pour into glass dish, rinsed in warm water, and sprinkle with a little sugar to prevent skin from forming on top. *Serve cold, with thin cream or milk.*

Prune Soufflé

½ lb. prunes   5 whites of eggs
½ cup sugar   ½ tablespoon butter

Soak prunes and cook until tender in a very little water. Remove stones, chop finely and mix with sugar. Stir in with a knife stiffly beaten whites. Pour into buttered soufflé—or baking-dish. Bake in moderate oven (385° F) for about 10 minutes. *Serve at once with whipped cream.* Serves 6.

Lemon Cream

1 small lemon (juice and grated rind)
⅔ cup sugar
4 tablespoons white wine
4 tablespoons water
5 yolks
1 cup cream

Rinse and dry lemon. Grate the rind into saucepan, add lemon juice, sugar, water, wine and yolks. Stir vigorously over the fire until the cream thickens, but *it must not boil*. Remove from fire and keep on stirring until cold, when it should be light and frothy. Add, if you like, a cupful of stiffly whipped cream. *Serve with macaroons*.

Delicious for cake filling, using half the quantity and leaving out the cream. Serves 6.

Red Wine Froth

1½ cups Burgundy or Claret
4 yolks
⅓ cup sugar
½ teaspoon finely grated lemon rind
1 tablespoon raspberry or red-currant jelly

Stir all ingredients over the fire until mixture thickens, but *it must not boil*. Remove from fire and keep on beating vigorously until cold. *Serve in glass dish or cream cups*. Serves 6.

Vanilla Cream

1 tablespoon gelatine
3 tablespoons water
1 egg
2 yolks
1 teaspoon vanilla extract
1½ cups cream
⅓ cup sugar
¾ cup milk

Soak gelatine in water and put into a saucepan together with egg, yolks, sugar, milk and vanilla. Stir briskly over

the fire until the mixture thickens, but *do not let it boil.*
Remove from fire and keep on beating until cold. Add
stiffly-whipped cream and pour into mould, rinsed in cold
water and sprinkled with sugar. Put in cold place to set.
Turn out and garnish with compôte and macaroons.

Half of the mixture could be colored green with pistachio kernels. Leave in the mould to set and then fill up
with the rest of the mixture. Serve with raspberry or
strawberry fruit sauce.

Chocolate, liqueur, arrack, coffee or lemon flavoring
could be used instead of the vanilla. Serves 6.

Moss Cream

5 yolks	½ lemon (grated rind and
⅔ cup Sherry	juice)
½ cup sugar	1 tablespoon gelatine
	1½ cups cream

Mix in a saucepan yolks, wine, sugar, lemon juice and
peel and stir briskly over the fire until mixture thickens,
but *it must not boil.* Soften gelatine in 3 tablespoons cold
water, add to hot mixture and remove from fire and keep
on beating until cold. Stir in gently hard-whipped cream.
Pour into mould, rinsed in cold water and sprinkled with
sugar. Stand in cold place to set. *Garnish with macaroons.*

Arrack Cream

2 cups cream	Sugar
6 yolks	Vanilla } To
1 tablespoon gelatine	Arrack, or cognac, } taste
	or rum

Boil cream with sugar. Beat yolks in basin, pour over cream and turn mixture into a saucepan. Beat vigorously over slow fire until it thickens, but *do not let it boil.* Soften gelatine in 3 tablespoons cold water and add to hot mixture. Remove from saucepan and keep on stirring for a few minutes. Add arrack, cognac, or rum and vanilla. Pour into mould, rinsed in cold water and sprinkled with sugar. *Serve with Fruit Syrup Sauce or compôte.* Serves 6.

Praline Cream

Cream:

4 yolks	1 tablespoon gelatine
2½ tablespoons sugar	1 cup thick cream
1 cup thin cream	

Praline:

Bare ⅔ cup sugar	⅓ cup almonds

To make praline, scald almonds and chop finely. Put sugar into a warmed frying pan, damp with a few drops water and stir with wooden spoon over the fire until dissolved. Add almonds, let it come to the boil and turn on to a buttered slab, or flat baking tin. When cool, cut into small squares with a buttered chopping knife.

Beat yolks and sugar well together. Boil thin cream and pour over mixture, stirring well. Return to saucepan, together with gelatine softened in cold water. Beat over the fire until cream thickens, but *it must not boil.* Pour into basin and keep on beating until heat is gone. When cold add chopped praline, and stir in gently hard-whipped cream. Pour into mould, rinsed in cold water and sprinkled with sugar, and stand in cold place to set. Serves 6.

Pineapple Cream

2 cups diced canned
  pineapples
4 yolks
⅓ cup sugar
2 tablespoons Sherry

4 tablespoons pineapple
  liquid
1 tablespoon gelatine
1 cup cream
1 white of egg

Cut one-quarter of the pineapples into small dice. Put into straining cloth and press out juice. Mix in a saucepan yolks, sugar, wine, pineapple liquid, and the white of egg. Stir briskly over the fire until the mixture thickens, but *it must not boil*. Add gelatine softened in 3 tablespoons cold water. Remove from the fire and keep on beating until cold. Add hard-whipped cream and, last of all, the pineapple dice. Pour into mould, rinsed in cold water and sprinkled with sugar. Stand in cold place until set. Turn out and garnish with the rest of the pineapple, cut into thin slices. Serves 6.

Chocolate Cream

1 egg
⅔ cup milk
5¼ tablespoons cocoa

1 cup sugar
1 tablespoon gelatine
1 cup thick cream

Put egg, milk, cocoa and sugar into a saucepan and beat well together. Add gelatine, softened in 3 tablespoons cold water. Beat vigorously over the fire until the mixture thickens, but *it must not boil*. Remove from saucepan and keep on beating until cold. Fold in hard-whipped cream gently. Pour into mould, rinsed in cold water and sprinkled with sugar. Put in cold place to set. Garnish with whipped cream. Serves 6.

Orange Cream

3 yolks	Grated rind of 1 orange
2½ tablespoons sugar	Juice of 4 oranges
1 cup thin cream	1 tablespoon gelatine
Grated rind of ½ lemon	1 cup thick cream

Mix in a saucepan yolks, sugar, thin cream and grated orange and lemon peel. Beat vigorously over the fire until mixture thickens, but *it must not boil*. Add gelatine softened in 3 tablespoons cold water. Remove from saucepan and keep on beating until cold. Add orange juice. Fold in whipped cream and pour into mould, rinsed in cold water and sprinkled with sugar. Leave in cold place to set. Serve with *Swedish Macaroons*. Serves 6.

Mock Cream Pudding

2 tablespoons butter	½ cup cold milk
2 cups milk	¼ teaspoon grated lemon
3 tablespoons sugar	peel
5 tablespoons flour	3–4 eggs

Baking-dish: ½ tablespoon butter.

Garnishing: 2 cups mashed cooked apples or jam.

Melt butter in a saucepan, add milk and sugar and let it come to the boil. While still boiling stir in flour mixed with ½ cup cold milk and cook for 3–4 minutes. Pour into basin and, when cool, stir in yolks, one at a time, add salt and fold in stiffly beaten whites with a knife. Pour into buttered baking-dish and leave in moderate oven (350° F) until half baked. Remove from oven, garnish quickly with mashed cooked apples or jam, sprinkle with sugar and return to oven, leaving it until fully baked. *Serve at once.* Serves 6.

Cream Cornets

2 eggs
$\frac{1}{2}$ cup sugar
$\frac{1}{2}$ cup flour

$\frac{1}{4}$ teaspoon ground
cinnamon

Beat eggs with sugar. Stir in flour and cinnamon. Put one tablespoonful on well-buttered baking tin, spread out into thin rounds and bake in moderate oven (385° F). When a nice color, shape into cornets while still hot. When cold fill with whipped cream, mixed with raspberry or strawberry jam. Makes 10.

BREADS AND BUNS

ALWAYS sift the flour.[1] Cold or damp flour should be spread in a warm place before using.

The liquid, used for doughs, should be heated to about 95° F. Cold liquid might be used, but in that case the dough should stand overnight, as it will take 10–14 hours to rise.

Fresh yeast should be creamy in color, should be brittle, and have a fresh—not sour—smell. Keep in a cool place.

Preparing a Dough

Put two-thirds of the flour and the salt into a mixing bowl. Stir the yeast with one teaspoon of sugar and 2 tablespoons of warm milk. Mix flour and yeast, adding the liquid gradually, warm or cold, according to the recipe. Work dough vigorously with a wooden spoon or with the hand, adding more flour, if necessary. When quite smooth and elastic sprinkle with flour and cover with a warm cloth. Stand in a warm place, away from draught, until the dough has risen to twice its size. Prepare the other ingredients in the meantime. Mix them with the dough, kneading vigorously, as before, work in more flour, if necessary, then leave again to rise. Remove dough to floured breadboard, knead well, roll out and make into loaves or buns, according to recipe. Arrange on lightly warmed greased tins, or floured cloth, cover with a cloth and leave to rise. Warm

[1] All purpose flour is used for all the recipes.

tins before greasing. Rub first with clean paper, then sparingly with cold butter, wrapped in a piece of thin cotton, or else use a butter wrapper.

The yeast yields the best results at 87–105° F, so be careful not to heat the liquid too much, or to stand the dough in too hot a place while rising.

Just before putting them into the oven brush the loaves, or buns, with lightly beaten egg. Brush rye bread with cold water, milk or beer.

When baked, put the bread on a cake cooler, or on a wooden board, covered by a cloth.

Ingredients Used for Bread and Cakes and How to Prepare Them

Fat: Cakes and bread, made with good unsalted butter are best in flavor. However, equal parts of butter and margarine or lard, gives very good results. The fat should be creamed with the sugar before being added to the dough.

Aniseed, Caraway Seed and Fennel Seed: Dry in cool oven and pound before adding to the mixture.

Cardamum: Dry in cool oven, peel, and pound seeds finely.

Saffron: Dry in cool oven (or it will lose its color), pound finely with a little sugar, mix with a little milk and add to the dough the second time it is being worked.

Bitter Orange Peel: Put on in cold water and boil, with the lid on, until soft. Remove white part and chop the rest, or cut into thin strips.

Almonds: Put into a basin, pour over boiling water and leave until the skins come off easily. *Never let almonds boil.* It makes them tough and spoils their flavor. Rinse under cold water and dry.

Toasted Almonds: Scald almonds, chop, or cut into thin strips. Toast under the grill, or roast in cool oven, or else fry in a pan over the fire. Stir often to avoid burning. Used for garnishing cakes, biscuits or sweets.

Pistachio Nuts: Scald and prepare as ordinary almonds.

Raisins: Rinse in several warm waters and dry well in a cloth.

Currants: Rinse in several warm waters, put under cold tap, dry well, pick, and mix with a little flour before adding to the dough.

Eggs: Whites will keep for several days in a cool place, if a little salt be added to them. When beating add a dash of cold water. A *yolk* will keep if put into a cup with cold water.

Essences of lemon, orange and bitter orange are made from the peel. Remove white parts, cut into thin strips and cover with rectified spirit, brandy or rum. Cover closely and leave for a fortnight. Strain and bottle, corking well.

Candied Orange Peel: Drain well and chop before adding to the mixture.

Fancy Yeast Bread

4¼ cups flour	¼ cup butter
2 yeast cakes	¼ cup sugar
1¼ cup milk	2 eggs
1 teaspoon salt	Chopped almonds

Crumble yeast into a bowl, slowly add the tepid milk and stir to dissolve the yeast. Add sugar, beaten eggs, salt and flour: mix, add the melted butter and mix very thoroughly. Turn out on floured board, knead into a smooth dough. Place in well-greased bowl. Cover and set aside to rise, let double in bulk (about 2 hours). Knead down and let rise 45 minutes or until it has doubled in bulk again.

Dark Bread

About 8 cups rye flour
About 4 cups white flour
3½ cups skim milk or sour milk
3 yeast cakes
2 teaspoons salt
1⅓ cups golden syrup

3 tablespoons finely-chopped bitter orange peel
2 tablespoons pounded fennel seed (not necessary)
¼ cup lard, or margarine and lard mixed

Work rye flour, part of the white flour, tepid milk and the yeast, mixed with the salt, into a dough. Leave to rise twice its size. Warm the syrup slightly, together with the lard and the condiments. Work into the dough, adding enough flour to make it rather firm. Leave again to rise. Remove to breadboard and work into it the rest of the flour. Divide into six portions. Work every portion separately until quite smooth and without any cracks. Roll into long loaves. Arrange on warmed blanket, covered by floured cloth, pulling up the cloth into a fold between each loaf. Cover with a cloth. When well risen arrange on slightly warmed greased tins, prick here and there with skewer, brush over with cold milk and bake in moderate oven (400° F) for about half an hour. When done, remove, brush over with warm water and leave for a while between blankets to keep crust soft.

Swedish Tin Loaves

About 8 cups coarse rye meal
About 3 cups white flour
2 teaspoons salt
1⅛ cups golden syrup

2 tablespoons pounded fennel seed (not necessary)
3½ cups cold milk
2 yeast cakes

Dissolve the yeast in a little cold milk. Sift the flour and mix with the condiments in a mixing bowl. Add the cold milk and work into a smooth dough. Add syrup and yeast and keep on working the dough. When quite smooth and glossy, cover with a cloth and leave in a fairly warm place to rise for 24 hours. Knead it again, then put it into greased and floured long cake tins, filling them not quite half-way up. Leave in warm place for the dough to rise to the top of the tins, then bake in fairly hot oven (425° F) to start with, and reduce to (385° F) after a while. When done, brush over with warm water, turn out and keep wrapped in a cloth until cold.

Rye Rounds

About 5 cups rye flour
About 3 cups white flour
2 cups skim milk
2 yeast cakes
2 teaspoons salt

½ tablespoon pounded fennel seed or aniseed
2 tablespoons fat
(2 tablespoons golden syrup)

Work rye flour, part of the white flour, tepid milk and the yeast, mixed with the salt, into a dough. Leave to rise to twice its size. Work in fennel seed, melted fat and warmed syrup, add more white flour, if necessary, and when well worked together, leave again to rise. Remove to breadboard, knead it again and divide into five portions, shaping each into a flat round. Prick all over with the prongs of a fork, and cut out a round in the middle with a paste cutter. Arrange on greased tins, and, when well risen, bake in hot oven (425° F).

Saffron Bread

About 7 cups white flour
2 cups milk
3 yeast cakes
1 teaspoon saffron
⅔ cup butter
¾ cup sugar
1 egg

2 tablespoons ground almonds
6 pounded bitter almonds
⅔ cup seeded raisins or ⅓ cup chopped candied peel

Coating:

1 egg
2 tablespoons chopped almonds

2 tablespoons granulated sugar

Work part of the flour, tepid milk and yeast into a dough. Leave to rise to twice its size. Dry saffron in very cool oven, pound finely with a little sugar, stir with a little milk and add to the dough. Cream sugar and butter and beat the egg. Work into the dough, together with almonds and raisins, previously soaked in warm water. Add more flour, if necessary, and, when well worked in, leave again to rise. Remove to floured breadboard, knead well and divide into 8 portions. Roll out, shape into strands and twist into a plait, which might be shaped into a wreath. Leave on greased tins to rise. Brush with lightly beaten egg and sprinkle with finely chopped almonds and sugar mixed. Bake in fairly hot oven (400° F).

Danish Buns

About 6 cups flour
½ cup sugar
2 cups cold milk
3 yeast cakes

6–8 cardamums (not necessary)
1¾ cups butter

Filling:

⅔ cup ground almonds   4 tablespoons butter
⅓ cup powdered sugar

Coating:

1 egg   ½ cup granulated sugar
4 tablespoons almonds

Sift flour into a bowl and mix with the sugar. Add milk gradually, also yeast, mixed with one teaspoon sugar. Add pounded cardamums and work dough into smooth and glossy consistency. Roll out on breadboard into good 1½ inches thickness. Dot butter all over. Fold in three, and then again in three, as you would a table napkin. Roll out again, fold as before. Repeat 3–4 times, or until the butter is well worked in. Leave for an hour in a cold place to get firm. In the meantime mix ground almonds well with sugar and butter and work into a smooth paste.

Roll the dough into ½ inch thickness, cut into ½ inch wide strips and twist two and two together, shaping them into rings or the figure 8. Put on buttered baking sheets, brush with lightly beaten egg, sprinkle with blanched, finely chopped almonds and leave to rise. When well risen sprinkle with sugar and bake in hot oven (450° F).

The rolled-out dough can also be cut into squares. Spread with a little almond paste, fold over the corners into an envelope, pressing down the edges, brush with egg and sprinkle with chopped almonds or hazel nuts. When baked, spread, if you like, with Icing (see page 146) flavored with a little vanilla or lemon juice.

Swedish Buns

2 cups flour   ½ cup milk
⅔ cup butter   1 egg
1½ tablespoons sugar   1 white of egg
1 yeast cake

Sift flour into bowl and mix with the sugar. Add milk gradually, also yeast, mixed with one teaspoon sugar, and work dough into smooth and glossy consistency. Roll out on breadboard into good $1\frac{1}{2}$-inch thickness. Dot butter all over, leaving a little for brushing buns with. Fold in three, and then in three again, as you would a table napkin. Roll out again, fold as before, repeating 3–4 times, or until the butter is well worked in. Leave for an hour in a cold place to get firm. Roll out on pastryboard, brush over with slightly warmed butter, cut into rounds, about $3\frac{1}{2}$ inches across, put a little jam, or chopped almonds, in the middle of each, fold over and brush over with lightly beaten white. Sprinkle with finely chopped almonds and granulated sugar. Leave on buttered tins to rise to twice their size. Bake in rather hot oven (425° F).

Semlor (Shrove Tuesday Buns)

In Sweden on Shrove Tuesday, and on every Tuesday during Lent, *"Semlor"* are served as pudding for dinner. They are eaten in soup plates, with hot milk flavored by blanched chopped almonds and a little vanilla sugar. Children especially are very fond of these Shrove Tuesday buns.

About 5 cups white flour	$\frac{2}{3}$ cup butter
2 cups milk	2 tablespoons almonds, of
3 yeast cakes	which 5 are bitter ones
1 cup sugar	

Coating: 1 egg.

Almond paste:

$\frac{1}{2}$ cup ground almonds	8 bitter almonds
1–2 tablespoons cold water	$2\frac{1}{4}$ cups powdered sugar

Sift flour into bowl, keeping some for the breadboard. Stir in tepid milk and the yeast, mixed with one teaspoon sugar. Work into smooth and glossy consistency. Leave, covered by cloth, to rise to twice its size. Stir butter and sugar into a froth, mix with blanched ground almonds and egg, and work well into the dough. Work in more flour, if necessary, then leave again to rise. Remove to breadboard, knead well and divide into 24 portions. Shape into round buns, arrange on well-greased tins, brush with lightly beaten egg and leave to rise quickly, preferably by placing tins over hot water. Bake in hot oven (450° F) for 10–15 minutes.

When cold, cut off the top from each bun, scoop out partly, fill with almond paste and replace the top. Dust with icing sugar.

For the *almond paste* work ground almonds with sugar and a little water into a smooth consistency. Five to six tablespoons hard-whipped cream, mixed in just before using the paste, makes it very delicious. Almond paste will remain fresh for several days, if rolled in icing sugar and kept well covered, in a cold place.

White Rusks

6 tablespoons lard	4 yeast cakes
3½ cups milk	⅔ cup butter
About 12 cups white flour	1 cup sugar

Melt the lard in the milk, which has the effect of making the rusks light and brittle. Sift flour into bowl, keeping some for the breadboard. Stir in tepid milk and lard mixture, also the yeast, mixed with one teaspoon sugar. Work into smooth and glossy consistency. Leave, covered by cloth, to rise to twice its size. Stir butter and sugar into a froth and work well into the dough, adding more flour, if necessary. Leave again to rise.

Remove to floured board, knead well and divide into 10 portions. Knead every portion well and cut into 25–30 pieces. Roll between the palms into little balls that should be absoluely smooth and glossy before putting on the greased baking tins. Cover with cloth and stand to rise in warm place, away from draught. Bake in hot oven (450° F) for a few minutes, then turn down the heat to 350° F. When a golden color remove and, when cold, slice in half and dry in very cool oven (325° F) until light brown on the surface, then in still cooler oven (250° F) until dry and brittle (about one hour).

Rye Rusks

6 tablespoons lard
3½ cups milk
4 cups rye flour
10 cups white flour
½ cup golden syrup
⅜ cup sugar
1–2 eggs

4 tablespoons finely chopped bitter orange peel
2 tablespoons fennel seed
2 teaspoons salt
⅔ cup butter
3 yeast cakes

Melt dripping in the milk which has the effect of making the rusks light and brittle. Sift flour into bowl, keeping some for the breadboard.. Stir in tepid milk and lard mixture, also the golden syrup and the yeast, mixed with one teaspoon sugar. Work into smooth and glossy consistency. Leave, covered by cloth, to rise to twice its size. Work in sugar, finely chopped bitter orange peel, pounded fennel seed, well-beaten eggs, creamed butter and more flour, if necessary. Knead well, then leave again to rise.

Remove to floured breadboard, knead well and divide into 12 portions. Knead every portion well and roll out into long thin loaves. Leave on greased tins to rise, then bake in fairly hot oven (400° F) for about 30 minutes. When a good color, remove and, when cold, cut into slices, about 1 inch in thickness, cut in half lengthwise, dry in very cool oven (325° F) until light brown on the surface, then in still cooler oven (250° F) until dry and brittle (about one hour).

CAKES AND COOKIES

Swedish Puff Paste

(For Bouchée, Vol-au-Vents, Fruit Tarts, etc.)

About 2 cups flour
4 tablespoons water
1 tablespoon Swedish
  Aquavit (or gin)

$\frac{1}{3}$ egg
$1\frac{1}{2}$ cups unsalted butter

Work flour, water, gin and egg lightly into a smooth paste. Roll out into a round of about 1-inch thickness. Put the butter in the middle, turning over the corners so as to cover the butter. Leave for 10 minutes, then (A) pat lightly with rolling pin into a square of about 1-inch thickness. Turn over the corners so as to meet in the middle (like an envelope), and fold new square in two. Repeat from (A) four times, then leave mixture in cold place for 15 minutes. Repeat again from (A) four times, then leave in cold place for one hour. Bake in hot oven (450° F).

Swedish Short Crust—I

$1\frac{3}{4}$ cups butter
About $3\frac{1}{2}$ cups flour
1 cup ground almonds

$\frac{1}{2}$ cup sugar
1 egg

Wash butter. Sift flour and work into a smooth paste together with the other ingredients. Leave for a couple of hours in a cold place before using. *Delicious foundation for fruit pies and tarts.*

145

Swedish Short Crust—II

2 cups flour
¾ cup butter
½ teaspoon salt

2 teaspoons sugar
4 tablespoons water
1 yolk

Sift flour. Work butter (which should be cold) lightly into the flour with the finger-tips. When quite smooth add salt, sugar, yolk and water quickly. Knead lightly, roll into a ball, wrap in a cloth and leave in cold place for an hour before using. *Delicious for pies, tarts and tartlets.*

Icing for Cakes—I

1 cup powdered sugar
2 tablespoons water

1 teaspoon lemon juice

Mix sugar with water and lemon juice. Stir until dissolved. Spread with a knife. When dry, garnish cake.

Icing for Cakes—II

1 cup powdered sugar

3 tablespoons wine
Liqueur or rum

Mix sugar with the liquid. Stir until dissolved. Spread with a knife. When dry, garnish cake.

Icing for Cakes—III

1 cup powdered sugar
1 white of egg

1 teaspoon lemon juice

Beat white lightly, add sugar and lemon juice, and stir until smooth and glossy. Spread with a knife and put into cool oven (325° F) for a minute to dry.

Zola Cake

Sponge cake:

1 egg	1½ tablespoons flour
1 yolk	1 teaspoon butter
1½ tablespoons sugar	

Marzipan:

2⅓ cups almonds	1 cup sugar

Zola Cream:

1 cup milk	3 tablespoons sugar
2 yolks	1 tablespoon gelatine
A few drops rum or vanilla extract	⅔ cup cream

Sponge Cake: Beat egg, yolk and sugar until light and creamy. Stir in flour and melted butter. Put a white paper on a baking tin, pour on the mixture and shape into a round, the same size as the cake tin to be used. Bake in slow oven (325° F) until light brown.

Marzipan: Work ground almonds and sugar well together and when nice and pliable roll out very thinly. Should the mixture not stick together add a little water or white of egg. Line a fairly wide cake tin with the marzipan and fill with Zola cream.

Zola Cream: Beat milk, yolks and sugar over a slow fire until mixture thickens, but *do not let it boil.* Remove from fire and stir in gelatine which was softened in 3 tablespoons cold water.

When cold fold in whipped cream and rum, or vanilla extract to taste.

Pour Zola cream into marzipan-lined tin. Place the sponge cake on top and leave until the cream has set. Turn out on a round dish and garnish with whipped cream, squeezed into a nice pattern with a piping tube.

Granny's Cake

4 eggs
8 tablespoons granulated
    sugar

½ grated lemon rind, or
    vanilla to taste
4 level tablespoons potato
    flour

Vanilla Cream:

4 yolks
2 tablespoons sugar

1 cup milk or cream
Vanilla essence to taste

Cake tin: 1 tablespoon butter, 2 tablespoons breadcrumbs.

Stir yolks with sugar until light and creamy. Add vanilla essence or grated lemon rind. Stir in gradually potato flour and add with a knife stiffly beaten whites. Pour into buttered and breadcrumbed cake tin and bake in moderate oven (400° F) for about 20 minutes.

When cold cut into three layers. Sandwich with vanilla cream and cover with icing, or whipped cream. Decorate with pieces of candied fruit, or slightly warmed red-currant jelly, using icing tube or paper funnel.

To make vanilla cream, beat yolks, sugar and milk (or thin cream) over slow fire until the mixture thickens, but *it must not boil.* Remove from fire, add vanilla essence and keep on beating until cold.

The cake could be sandwiched with apricot paste, or mashed cooked apples, instead of with vanilla cream.

Crown Cake

½ cup butter
1 cup sugar
3 eggs

1½ cups grated cold
    potatoes
2⅓ ground almonds

Cake tin: 1 tablespoon butter, 2 tablespoons breadcrumbs.

Wash and dry butter. Stir for 15 minutes with sugar, yolks and grated potatoes. Stir in almonds and stiffly beaten whites. Pour into buttered and breadcrumbed cake tin and bake in moderate oven (385° F). When a nice color, remove from oven and leave for 10–15 minutes before turning out. Pour over Lemon Sauce or Wine Sauce.

Almond Cake

$2\frac{1}{3}$ cups ground almonds   4 whites of eggs
1 cup sugar

Cake tin: 1 tablespoon butter, 2 tablespoons breadcrumbs.

Mix almonds and sugar well together, stir in stiffly beaten whites with a knife, and pour into buttered and breadcrumbed savarin mould. Bake in fairly cool oven (325° F). When cold, fill the hole in the middle with raspberry or strawberry compôte. *Serve with Vanilla Sauce.*

Mazarin Cake

Shortpaste:

About $1\frac{3}{4}$ cups flour   1 small egg
$\frac{1}{2}$ cup butter   1 teaspoon baking
$\frac{1}{3}$ cup sugar   powder

Filling:

1 cup ground almonds $\frac{1}{2}$ cup butter
1 cup confectioner's   2 eggs
   sugar   Raspberry jam

Wash butter, if salted. Sift flour and baking powder. Mix shortcake ingredients well together on the breadboard and work into smooth consistency.

Filling:

Add one egg at a time, stirring well. Work sugar, almonds and butter into a smooth paste. Line buttered and breadcrumbed cake tin with short-paste. Cover with layer of jam, spread filling on top and bake in fairly cool oven (325° F) for about $\frac{1}{2}$ hour.

Alexander Tart

Shortpaste:

1½ cups butter   3 tablespoons sugar
2½ cups flour   1 egg

Filling: 1 cup mashed cooked apples.

Almond paste:

2⅔ cups ground almonds   3 whites of eggs
1⅓ cups powdered sugar

Wash and dry butter, and stir until white and creamy. Stir egg and sugar well together and mix with butter. Stir in sifted flour. Leave in cold place for an hour or so.

Spread bottom of round cake tin, or Swedish cast-iron frying pan, with fairly thin layer of short paste. Bake in moderate oven (385° F), then leave to cool. Now line the sides of the cake tin with shortpaste, and filled with mashed cooked apples.

Almond paste: Mix ground almonds and sugar well together, and stir in lightly beaten whites. Spread almond paste over the apples.

Roll out the rest of the shortpaste and cut into strips with a pastry cutter. Arrange in a crisscross pattern on top of the cake. Now edge the cake with a thin band of short-paste. Bake in moderate oven (385° F) and *serve with whipped cream or vanilla sauce.*

Nougat Cakes

Shortpaste:

⅓ cup butter	2 tablespoons sugar
1 cup flour	2½ tablespoons ground
1 yolk	almonds

Cream filling:

1 egg	1 tablespoon sugar
4 tablespoons cream	Vanilla extract

Nougat:

1½ cups sugar	2 tablespoons boiling
¼ cup almonds	water

Mix butter, flour, sugar and almonds into a paste with the finger-tips. Add yolk, and work with wooden spoon until quite smooth. Leave for about an hour in a cold place. Line fluted patty tins with paste. Roll out the rest of the paste thinly and cut into rounds, the same size and number as the cakes (about eight or nine). Bake a nice color in moderate oven (385° F).

Cream filling: Beat well egg, cream and sugar in saucepan, put on the slow fire and keep on beating until mixture thickens, but *do not let it boil*. Remove from fire and keep on beating until fairly cool. Add vanilla extract. Fill patties with the cream, put the pastry rounds on top, and turn upside-down.

Nougat: Blanch and chop almonds finely. Put sugar into a well-cleaned small frying pan and stir evenly with a wooden spoon over the fire. When sugar starts melting, lower the heat to prevent it from scorching. When a golden brown, add boiling water and almonds, and pour mixture quickly over the cakes. Should the nougat harden in the pan, heat again, but be careful not to let it turn too brown.

Lemon Cakes

4 eggs   ⅓ cup potato flour
⅓ cup powdered sugar

Lemon cream filling:

1 egg   4 tablespoons milk
1 tablespoon sugar   Lemon juice and peel to
                                          taste

Icing: 4 tablespoons powdered sugar, water.

Garnishing: ½ white, icing sugar, coloring.

Stir yolks and sugar until light and creamy, mix in potato flour with a knife, also the beaten whites. Butter some fairly large patty tins, and sprinkle with flour. Fill almost to the top with mixture and bake in fairly hot oven (400° F). Turn out and when cold, cut in half, sandwich with lemon cream, put halves together, cover with icing and pipe a nice pattern on top with ½ white, mixed with powdered sugar and colored with carmine, or green coloring. Or else put a strip of candied orange peel on top.

Lemon cream: Beat well in a saucepan egg, sugar and milk, put on a slow fire and keep on beating until mixture thickens, but *do not let it boil.* Remove from fire and keep on beating until cold. Add lemon juice and grated lemon peel to taste.

Walnut Cake

6 eggs   1 cup ground walnuts
1 cup sugar   ½ cup potato flour
2 tablespoons water

Cake tin: ½ tablespoon butter, 2 tablespoons bread crumbs.

Garnishing and filling: 1 cup cream, 1 cup walnuts.

Separate yolks and whites. Stir yolks briskly with sugar for at least 15 minutes, adding at intervals the water. Stir in potato flour and walnuts. Add stiffly beaten whites, mixing carefully with a knife. Pour into buttered and bread-crumbed cake tin and bake in moderate oven (350° F).

When cold cut cake in half and sandwich with whipped cream, mixed with $\frac{1}{2}$ cup finely chopped walnuts. Cover cake with whipped cream and garnish with whole walnuts.

Napoleon Cake

3$\frac{1}{3}$ cups ground almonds   1$\frac{1}{4}$ cups butter
1$\frac{3}{4}$ cups powdered sugar   2$\frac{1}{2}$ cups flour

Filling: Mashed cooked apples or red-currant jelly.

Garnishing: Icing or whipped cream, and candied fruit.

Mix sugar and ground almonds well together. Wash and dry butter, and stir until white and creamy. Work into it almond paste and flour. Divide into three parts and roll out into fairly thin rounds. Arrange on baking tins or use Swedish cast-iron pancake pan, and bake in fairly hot oven (400° F). When cool, sandwich with mashed cooked apples, red-currant jelly or vanilla cream. Cover with icing or whipped cream, and garnish with pieces of candied fruit.

Ambrosia Cake

3 eggs   1 cup butter
1 cup sugar   1 cup flour

Garnishing: Icing, 2–3 candied orange peel or 1$\frac{1}{2}$ tablespoons almonds.

Stir eggs and sugar for 20 minutes. Stir in melted butter and flour. Pour into one large, or two smaller, buttered and breadcrumbed cake tins, and bake in moderate oven (385° F) for about ½ hour.   Turn out and, when cooled, spread with icing and sprinkle with finely chopped candied orange peel or scalded, lightly roasted almonds, cut into strips.

Swedish Ginger Cake

2 cups flour	1 tablespoon ground
2 cups brown sugar	cinnamon
2 tablespoons chopped	1½ teaspoons baking
bitter orange peel	powder
1 tablespoon ground	2 eggs
cloves	1 cup milk
	3 tablespoons butter

Cake tin: ½ tablespoon butter, 2 tablespoons breadcrumbs.

Boil bitter orange peel, cut away the white part and chop the rest finely. Mix sifted flour, baking powder, sugar, ground condiments and bitter orange peel.   Beat eggs well, add milk and stir slowly into the dry mixture. Stir in melted butter.   When well mixed pour into buttered and breadcrumbed cake tin, or Swedish cast-iron frying pan, and bake in moderate oven (385° F) for 30–40 minutes.

Chopped candied peel could be used instead of the bitter orange peel.

Cake à la Bennich

1 cup ground almonds	1 cup powdered sugar
4 whites of eggs	

Filling:

¾ cup powdered sugar	4 tablespoons cream
4 yolks	⅔ cup fresh butter

Beat whites into hard froth and stir in ground almonds and sugar. Pour into two buttered sandwich tins and bake in cool oven (325° F).

Filling: Beat sugar, cream and yolks in a saucepan over a slow fire until it thickens, but *do not let it boil.* Remove from fire and, when cooled, stir in butter. Sandwich the cakes with the cream filling and spread some of it on top. Sprinkle with toasted almond strips. *A delicious sweet.*

Tosta de Benici Cake

5 eggs	1 cup butter
Flour enough to make mixture the consistency of a thick porridge	1¼ cups sugar ½ cup almonds 10 bitter almonds

Stir slightly warmed butter until white and creamy. Mix with yolks, sugar, and scalded and ground bitter almonds. Cut unskinned ordinary almonds into thin strips and add to the mixture. Stir in flour and last of all add with a knife hard-beaten whites. Pour into well-buttered savarin mould. Bake in hot oven (100° F) but do not look at the cake for the first 24 minutes.

Mazarins

Shortpaste:

5 tablespoons butter	½ teaspoon baking powder
⅓ cup powdered sugar	
1 yolk	Butter for patty tins
About ¾ cup flour	

Almond filling:

Bare ¾ cup ground almonds	2 eggs
	1 cup powdered sugar

Icing: 7 tablespoons powdered sugar, water.

Wash butter and dry. Stir with sugar into creamy consistency. Stir in yolk. Sift flour and baking powder and stir into mixture. Leave in cold place for at least an hour.

Almond filling: Mix ground almonds well with eggs and sugar, stirring for a few minutes.

Line buttered patty tins with a shortpaste, fill with almond mixture and bake in moderate oven (385° F). When cooled cover filling with icing, and return to cool oven (325° F) for a few minutes.

The Professor's Cookies

2 eggs
1 cup sugar
1½ squared bitter chocolate

½ cup butter
½ cup almonds
½ cup flour

Beat eggs and sugar until light and creamy. Flake chocolate and melt with the butter. Mix with the eggs and sugar. Add blanched and coarsely chopped almonds. Stir in flour. Bake at once in two well-buttered long cake tins. Cut in half lengthwise, and cut each half into 10 slices.

Almond Patties

⅞ cup butter
2 cups flour
¾ cup sugar

2 yolks
1 cup ground almonds
10 bitter almonds

Wash and dry butter. Divide into lumps and mix with sifted flour, sugar, yolks, ground almonds and blanched and chopped bitter almonds. Work into a smooth paste and stand in cold place for 2 hours. Shape into thin roll, divide into equal portions and line patty tins. Place on a baking tin and bake in fairly cool oven (325° F). When a golden brown remove from oven, turn out patties, and leave to get cold on the patty tins turned upside-down. It can be used quite plain, or filled with jam, or mashed cooked apples, with whipped cream on top. They could also have meringe mixture on top. Sprinkle with sugar and put into moderate oven (350° F) for a few minutes, or until the meringue has turned a light yellow.

Pancake Cookies

6 tablespoons melted butter
½ cup sugar
2 eggs

¾ cup flour
½ cup almonds
2 tablespoons pearl sugar

Melt butter and stir until white and creamy. Stir eggs and sugar well together and add the butter. Stir in sifted flour. Blanch almonds, chop, and mix with coarsely grained sugar. Heat the "plättpanna" or pancake pan. Brush with melted butter and fill each round with ½ tablespoon of the mixture. Sprinkle with almonds and sugar and bake in moderate oven (385° F). When a nice color roll at once round a broom handle or heavy stick.

Sand Cookies

1 cup butter
2½ cups flour
1 teaspoon vanilla extract

½ cup sugar
2-3 teaspoons baking powder

Brown the butter in a saucepan and stir until cold. Stir in the other ingredients and work into a smooth paste. Shape into tiny buns. Arrange on buttered tin and bake in moderate oven (380° F).

Finnish Coffee Fingers

1 cup butter
2 tablespoons sugar
6 bitter almonds, grated

2½ cups flour
Salt

Coating: 1 beaten egg, ½ cup finely chopped almonds.

Cream butter, add sugar gradually, almonds, then flour, and set in cool place for 1 hour. Roll out to finger thickness, cut into strips about 2 inches long, brush with beaten egg, roll in almonds, place on baking sheet and bake in moderate oven (385° F) until golden brown. (Makes about 70 cookies).

Butter Rings

3 cups flour
2 cups butter

10 tablespoons cream

Coating: ¾ cup sugar, ¼ cup cinnamon.

Mix flour, butter and cream to a smooth dough and roll out about ⅓-inch thick. Cut out rings by using a big and small glass and bake in moderate oven (385° F). When light brown dip them in the coating mixture. *Delicious with light desserts.*

Old Fashioned Ginger Snaps

1 cup butter
1 cup molasses
1 cup sugar
1 cup cream
1 teaspoon cinnamon

1 teaspoon cloves
1 teaspoon bicarbonate of soda
2 teaspoons baking powder

Mix all ingredients except sugar and baking powder to a smooth dough and let stand 24 hours. Roll on floured board and cut with biscuit cutter. Before baking add the

sugar and baking powder. Bake in fairly hot oven
(425° F).

Dreams

1 cup sugar
1 cup fresh butter
2½ cups flour

½ teaspoon bicarbonate of
soda
½ teaspoon cream of tartar
2 teaspoons vanilla extract

Mix all ingredients well together on a breadboard. Roll
into small balls and bake in slow oven (325° F).

Brandy Rings

1¾ cups butter
1 cup sugar

1 wineglass brandy
5½ cups flour

Wash and dry butter. Sift flour. Mix all ingredients
into smooth paste on a pastryboard. Roll into very thin
lengths, twist two and two together like a string, cut into
pieces of about 6 inches and shape into circlets. Bake in
moderate oven (385° F).

Uppåkra Cookies

1¾ cups butter
1 cup sugar

2 cups potato flour
3½ cups flour

Coating:

2 eggs
4 tablespoons almonds

⅓ cup pearl sugar

Wash and dry the butter. Stir well with sugar and work
in potato and ordinary flour. Roll out thinly on breadboard and cut into small rounds. Fold over almost in the
middle, brush with beaten egg and sprinkle with chopped

almonds and sugar.   Bake to a nice color in hot oven (425° F).

Almond Cookies

1¼ cups butter
1 cup sugar
1 egg

3 tablespoons bitter
    almonds
3 cups flour

Wash and dry butter.   Mix well with sugar, egg, flour and blanched and grated bitter almonds.   Work into smooth paste.   Press through large piping tube, cut lengths of about 5 inches, and shape like an "S," or just a circlet. Bake in moderate oven (385° F).

Oat Cookies

½ cup butter
1 cup sugar

2 cups Quaker oats
2 whites of eggs

Melt butter and mix well with sugar and oats.   Add stiffly beaten whites.   Shape with teaspoon into little balls. Bake on buttered tins in moderate oven (385° F).

Jew Cookies

½ cup butter
½ cup brown sugar
1 teaspoon ground
    cinnamon
1 teaspoon baking powder

3 pounded cardamums
    (not necessary)
5 grated bitter almonds
1 egg
About 2 cups flour

Coating:

1 white of egg
2 tablespoons granulated
    sugar

½ teaspoon ground
    cinnamon

Wash and dry butter. Stir with sugar for 15 minutes. Work in egg, bitter almonds, cardamums and last of all sifted flour, mixed with baking powder. Leave in cold place for 2 hours. Roll out very thinly and cut into small rounds. Brush with lightly beaten white and sprinkle with sugar and cinnamon mixed. Bake in moderate oven (385° F).

Jam Cookies

1 cup butter
½ cup sugar
1 yolk

2¾ cups pastry flour
6 tablespoons raspberry jam

Coating:

1 white of egg
2 tablespoons almonds

2 tablespoons pearl sugar

Wash butter and stir with sugar until light and creamy. Stir in yolk and flour and work into smooth consistency. Leave in cold place overnight if possible. Roll out very thinly, and cut into rounds with a pastry cutter. Spread half with jam, and fold over. Brush with lightly beaten white, sprinkle with finely chopped almonds and sugar mixed. Bake in moderate oven (385° F).

Swedish Macaroons

2 cups ground almonds
2 sheets wafer paper

1½ cups powdered sugar
2 whites of eggs

Icing:

1 large white of egg
Bare 1 cup powdered sugar

1 teaspoon lemon juice

Garnishing:

2 tablespoons almonds
1 tablespoon pistachio
  nuts

1½ oz. candied orange
  peel
1½ oz. mixed candied
  peel

Cut the wafer papers into oblongs (3½ x 1½ inches). Work almonds, sugar and whites into a smooth paste. If too hard add more white. Spread fairly thin layer of paste on the wafer papers, and bake in cool oven (300° F) until they are a light yellow, hard and dry on the surface, but soft inside. Remove from oven and, when cool, spread with icing, and sprinkle with blanched and chopped almonds, chopped pistachio nuts, and finely chopped peel, all well mixed. Put them back into the oven, and leave until the icing has dried, and is a nice cream color. *Delicious.*

Oatmeal Biscuits

¾ cup oatmeal
1¼ cups white flour
1½ teaspoons baking
  powder

1½ tablespoons water
½ cup butter
½ cup sugar
1 egg

Sift flour and mix well with baking powder. Stir butter with sugar until white and creamy. Add flour, the well-beaten egg, and water, and work into smooth consistency. Leave for 2 hours in cold place. Roll out very thin, prick all over with the prongs of a fork, cut into fairly large rounds, and bake on buttered baking tins in moderate oven (385° F). *Serve, buttered, with jam or marmalade.*

Swedish Crisp Biscuits

1¾ cups white flour
2 cups coarse rye meal or rye flour
1 tablespoon sugar

1 teaspoon salt
½ cup butter
1 cup milk

Sift flour into mixing bowl and mix with sugar and salt. Divide butter into portions and dot over flour. Rub in well with the finger-tips, add milk gradually, until you have a fairly firm dough. Work well into smooth and glossy consistency. When the dough comes away from the sides of the bowl, roll out very thinly, prick all over with the prongs of a fork, and cut (using a ruler) into oblongs (4 x 2½ inches). Bake on buttered tins a nice golden brown in moderate oven (385° F). *A delicious substitute for toast.*

PRESERVES

Ginger Pears

5–6 lbs. medium-sized
  cooking pears
2 lbs. sugar

2 cups water
3–4 pieces ginger

Peel pears and cut a cross at the top of each. Put the fruit and sugar in layers in preserving pan and add water. Add ginger, slightly crushed and wrapped in a piece of muslin. Simmer gently until liquid is quite clear, or about 4 hours. Remove carefully to a large flat dish. When cold put into jars, rinsed with brandy. Remove ginger from syrup, slightly condense by boiling a little longer and when cold, pour over pears which should be absolutely cold before covering the jars. Add a little ground ginger if flavor is too insipid.

Served as sweet with whipped cream.

Cranberry Pears

7 cups cranberries
5 cups water
1¾ lbs. sugar

5–6 lbs. medium-sized
  cooking pears

Pick cranberries carefully, rinse and put them on in cold water. Simmer until reduced almost to pulp. Leave to strain through jelly bag or fine cloth. Boil gently with sugar until quite clear. Skim well.

Peel pears, cut in two lengthwise, remove cores, scrape stalks, and put into the syrup. Simmer gently, uncovered, until they are quite tender and syrup looks clear. Remove carefully to large flat dish and, when cooled, put into jars, rinsed in brandy. If necessary, reduce syrup by boiling a little longer. When quite cold, pour over pears. Cover jars with parchment paper.

Served as a sweet with whipped cream.

Cranberry apples are treated in the same way.

Orange Peel Preserves

2 lbs. boiled orange peel (yellow part)
3½ cups sugar

2 cups orange peel liquid
1 teaspoon citric acid

Soak orange peel in water for three days, changing the water every day. Put on in boiling water and cook, covered, until quite soft. Remove and drain on cloth. Weigh peels. Boil sugar, orange peel liquid and citric acid into a clear syrup. Put in orange peels and simmer gently for about 20 minutes, remove to earthenware jars and keep on boiling syrup until fairly thick. Pour, while still hot, over the peels. When cold cover jars with parchment paper. Should the syrup turn sugary, reboil with a little water, skim well and, when cold, pour over peels.

Delicious for garnishing cakes and sweets.

Dried Orange Peel

Put ordinary—or Seville—orange peel in a warm place, on the plate rack of a gas stove for instance, or else in an airy place. Dry them well, or they will not keep. When wanted, put on in cold water and boil, covered, until soft. Remove inner pith, leaving only the outer rind.

Used for flavoring bread, rusks, etc.

Pickled Gherkins

50 white or green gherkins
1 tablespoon cream of
  tartar
1 teaspoon alum
1¾ cups kitchen salt
4½ quarts water

3½ cups white wine
  vinegar
Cherry or red-currant
  leaves
Dill
1 cup horseradish, cut into
  pieces

Brush gherkins and soak in cold water overnight. Pound cream of tartar and alum with salt, add to the water and leave for 24 hours. Remove gherkins, drain and leave on a sheet, folded in two, to dry for 3 hours. Arrange in layers in wooden tub, or large stone jar, with cherry or red-currant leaves, sprigs of dill and horseradish between each layer. The gherkins must not touch each other, or the sides of the vessel, as it turns them spotty. Wrap each gherkin in a leaf and make top and bottom layer of leaves. Add vinegar to the pickle and pour gently over gherkins which should be well covered by liquid. Put a wooden board, with a light weight on top, over the jar and stand in a cool place for 3–4 weeks, before using. Keep an eye on them occasionally to make sure that the gherkins are well covered by pickle. Should they turn mildewy, add more vinegar and salt mixed.

They are served, sliced, with roast meat and game.

Pickled Cucumber

1 large cucumber

2 tablespoons salt

Pickle:

⅓ cup vinegar
1 tablespoon water
2 tablespoons sugar

½ teaspoon white pepper
2 tablespoons finely
  chopped parsley

Peel cucumber and cut into thin slices, starting from the stalk end. Arrange in layers, with salt in between, on a dinner plate, put another on top, right side up, and leave, with weights on top, for a couple of hours. Pour away the juice.

Mix vinegar, water, sugar and pepper, put the cucumber into the pickle and serve in glass dish, sprinkled with finely chopped parsley.

Delicious with roast chicken or veal.

Pickled Silver Onions

2 lbs. button onions	7 cups white wine
7 cups water	5 mace leaves
4 tablespoons salt	1 cup sugar

Peel onions under running water to keep your eyes from smarting. Soak in salt and water for 24 hours. Boil half of the vinegar with mace and sugar. Put in onions and simmer gently until they are clear and tender, taking 5–10 minutes. Remove onions and put into a jar. Pour the rest of the vinegar over the onions, cover with a folded cloth and put a plate on top. When quite cold, cover jar with parchment paper.

Serve with roast meat or game.

Pickled Beets

Wash beets well. Put on in cold water, with a little salt, or sugar, and simmer until tender. Remove beets and when cold, peel, cut into thin slices and arrange in a jar in layers, with sugar in between. Cover well with vinegar (or lemon juice) mixed with sugar ($1\frac{1}{2}$ tablespoons sugar to 1 cup vinegar). Keep the jar uncovered to prevent the beets from turning mildewy. A few horseradish shavings and a few cloves add a nice flavor to the pickle.

The best way to prepare the beets is to bake them in the oven as you do potatoes.

In hot weather it is better to use cold *boiled* vinegar for the pickle.

Pickled Tomatoes

10 green unripe tomatoes   5 cups water
2 cups vinegar

Pickle:

2 lbs. sugar   10 cloves
$\frac{2}{3}$ cup vinegar $\frac{1}{4}$ chili pepper
4 cups water

Wipe tomatoes with a damp cloth and prick all over with a little silver fork. Boil water and vinegar, pour over tomatoes and leave for 24 hours.

To make pickle boil vinegar, water, sugar and condiments into a clear syrup. Put in tomatoes and simmer until tender. Remove and put into glass jars. Should the syrup not be thick enough, keep on boiling a little longer before pouring it over the tomatoes. Cover jam with parchment paper.

FRUIT SYRUPS

FRUIT syrups serve many purposes in a Swedish home. Diluted with cold water they are the children's favorite drink, especially in the summer, when on returning from a strenuous game or lovely bath, nothing could look more tempting than a jug of ruby-colored raspberry syrup, or golden orange syrup, with chunks of ice tinkling against the glass, and platefuls of those delicious biscuits and buns I have described in this book. A Swedish mother also finds these fruit drinks invaluable for children's parties and picnics.

Fruit syrups are also used for making cold fruit soups, fruit syrup cream and sauces to go with sweet puddings and creams.

Here are a few tips when making fruit syrups:

Ripe fruit yields more juice and gives a richer flavor. Boil quickly to prevent the syrup from setting into a jelly.

Unsweetened syrup should be poured hot into heated bottles.

Cork at once and seal bottles with resin or paraffin. Soak the corks in boiling water and dry on clean towel before using.

Melt resin with sealing-wax and ordinary wax (7 oz. resin, 1 oz. sealing-wax, $\frac{1}{4}$ oz. ordinary wax). Dip the neck of the bottle into the mixture 2–3 times.

Paraffin can also be used for sealing the bottles. Stand a jar of paraffin in boiling water until melted, then mix with vinegar (7 oz. paraffin to one teaspoonful of vinegar).

Raspberry Syrup

7 pints raspberries
3 cups water

1½ cups sugar to each lb. of
raspberry juice

Pick and rinse fruit, crush and put on in preserving pan together with cold water. Let it come to the boil quickly, stirring, then simmer for 15 minutes. Leave to run through jelly bag, or fine cloth, until next day. Weigh the juice, add sugar, allowing 1½ cups to each lb. of juice, and, when dissolved, boil briskly for about 10 minutes, skimming carefully all the time. Bottle, when cold (see page 169).

Red Currant Syrup

7 pints red currants
3 cups water

1½ cups sugar to each lb. of
red currant juice

For making syrup, see Raspberry Syrup above.

Black Currant Syrup

7 pints black currants
7 cups water

12 oz. sugar to each lb. of
black currant juice

For making syrup, see Raspberry Syrup above.

Cherry Syrup

12 lbs. sound cooking
cherries

6 lbs. granulated sugar

Remove stalks, but leave the stones. Rinse and drain well. Put layers of cherries and sugar in a stone jar, cover with plate and make airtight by sticking edges together with a paste of rye flour and water. Stand in pan with cold water, let it come to the boil slowly, and steam for 6 hours from the time water boils. Add more water to the pan so that it overlaps the cherries in the jar all the time. When cooked pour into jelly bag, or thin cloth, and leave to strain until next day. Bottle cold.

Dry the cherries in very cool oven, or on the hot plate rack, and make into fruit syrup cream by boiling with water and sugar, and thickening with potato flour. (See page 127.)

Raspberry Syrup with Red Currants

16 pints raspberries
7 cups red currants
Bare 15 cups water

2 cups sugar to each lb. of fruit juice

Pick raspberries and strip the currants from the stalks. Put on in cold water and boil into a pulp, stirring all the time. Pour into jelly bag, or thin cloth, and leave to strain until next day. Weigh juice and boil with sugar until quite clear and the consistency of a syrup. Bottle hot or cold.

Orange Syrup—I

6 oranges
$5\frac{1}{2}$ lbs. sugar

$5\frac{1}{2}$ cups water
$1\frac{1}{4}$ oz. citric acid

Wash and wipe oranges. Grate off yellow rind and put into a jar, together with sugar, orange juice and finely pounded citric acid. Cover jar and leave for 4 days, stirring now and again. Strain and pour into dry bottles. Cork and seal.

Orange Syrup—II

6 oranges   5½ cups water
4½ lbs. granulated sugar   1¼ oz. citric acid

Wash and wipe oranges. Peel and remove the pith. Cut yellow part into thin strips and put into a jar, together with boiling water. Cover with kitchen rubber, folded in four, put a plate on top and leave for 3 days. Pour into jelly bag and leave to strain. Add sugar and finely pounded citric acid. Stir for about one hour, or until the sugar has melted and the syrup is quite clear. Pour into dry bottles. Cork and seal.

CONFECTIONERY

Swedish Toffee (Kola)

1 tablespoon butter
2 cups thin cream
⅔ cup brown sugar
2¾ cups white sugar

½ cup cocoa
¾ cup golden syrup
1 tablespoon vanilla sugar

Pour all the ingredients into an iron saucepan stirring evenly until a little of the mixture turns tough when dropped into cold water. Pour at once on a well-buttered baking tin. When cooled cut into 1 inch squares. Wrap in wax paper.

Knäck

2 cups cream
3 cups sugar
2 cups golden syrup

1¼ cups almonds
4 tablespoons breadcrumbs

Scald almonds and chop finely. Pour cream, syrup and sugar into saucepan, stirring evenly until a little of the mixture turns almost hard when dropped into cold water (about 25 minutes). Add breadcrumbs and boil for 5 minutes. Stir in almonds and let the mixture come to the boil quickly. Pour into little fluted paper cases.

Jockey Caps

Almond paste:

1 cup ground almonds	1 white of egg
1 cup powdered sugar	Red and green coloring

Coating:

1½ cups sugar	1 teaspoon vinegar
4 tablespoons water	

Mix ground almonds, sugar and white into a smooth paste. Divide into three portions. Color one with carmine, another with green coloring and leave the third uncolored. Shape into balls, the size of a small marble.

Pour sugar, water and vinegar into saucepan and boil, without stirring, into pale golden color. Test with a match, dipping same in cold water, then in mixture, then in cold water. When hard and brittle the mixture is ready for use. Drop balls, one at a time, and remove carefully with a teaspoon, without stirring mixture. Put jockey caps on well-buttered baking tin.

Keep in covered jar in dry place.

BEVERAGES

Chocolate

2 cups milk	4 tablespoons cocoa
2 cups water	1 tablespoon potato flour
2 squares bitter chocolate	4 tablespoons sugar

Serving: ⅔ cup cream.

Break chocolate into a saucepan. Add milk and water and let it come to the boil. Stir cocoa and potato flour with a little cold water. Add to the boiling liquid, beating well. When boiling, add sugar to taste. The chocolate should be like a thin syrup.

Serve hot in cups, with a dash of very cold stiffly whipped cream, flavored with a little vanilla sugar, on top. Serves 6.

Swedish Punsch

Most people seem to have heard about *Punsch*, a Swedish liqueur that nowadays is really more popular with visitors to my country than with the Swedes themselves. It has a sweet rather innocent taste, and inexperienced Germans, coming over to Sweden, are said to have been wont to drink it in tankards, in their own native fashion, being greatly surprised when they wake up the next morning with a headache.

Punsch can be made in several different ways. I shall give you two to select from:

175

9 pints water
5½ lbs. powdered sugar
2 whole bottles arrack
1 whole bottle fairly good
  brandy

1 whole bottle 95%
  spirit
2 teaspoons turpentine

Put sugar and water in preserving pan and reduce by boiling into 9 pints syrup. Allow to cool. Mix with other ingredients. Keep on ladling the *punsch* for one hour. Bottle, cork and seal bottles, and keep in a lying position. Improves with time, but can be used after 2 days.

Swedish Punsch (Another way)

4½ quarts water
13 lbs. preserving sugar
7½ whole bottles best
  arrack

¼ bottle whisky
½ bottle dark sherry

Boil water and sugar for 2 minutes in preserving pan. Skim well. When cold, stir in arrack, whisky and sherry. Keep on ladling the *punsch* for a full hour. Bottle, cork and seal bottle, and keep in a lying position. Improves with time, but can be used after 2 days.

Swedish Glögg

Glögg brings to your mind visions of a Swedish Christmas, with snow and cold outside, and the family gathering round a crackling fire at home, drinking the health of those near and dear ones who have to spend their Christmas in the far corners of the world. A Swedish sleigh-party without *Glögg* to warm them after the long drive through snow-plowed forest, would be unthinkable.

This drink can be made in several different ways. Here is a good recipe:

1 whole bottle domestic
  brandy
1 wine glass port, madeira,
  or burgundy
1 cup sugar

Small piece cinnamon
10 cardamums
10 cloves
A handful raisins and
  blanched almonds

Put brandy, condiments, almonds and raisins in a saucepan. Heat slightly. Put the sugar on a cake cooler over the saucepan. Put a match to the brandy, and while burning keep on ladling the spirit over the sugar until it has all melted. Remove the grid at once and cover the saucepan. Add the wine before serving. *Serve hot, with a few almonds and raisins in each glass.*

Glögg should be kept in well-corked and sealed bottles. Heat, *but do not boil,* before using.

The following is another favorite:

Glögg (Another way)

2 bottles Sherry (domestic)
½ bottle brandy (domestic)
5 pieces citrus peel
¾ cup almonds

5 pieces cinnamon
10 cloves
1 cup raisins

Cook the spices in enough wine to cover them, for 15 minutes. Bottle with the rest of wine and brandy and leave it for a few days before serving. It will keep indefinitely. *Always serve hot.*

INGREDIENTS USED IN SWEDISH COOKING

HERE is a list of ingredients, used in Swedish cooking. They are quite inexpensive and you can get them at most leading stores:

ARRACK—a characteristic Swedish distilled spirit

BITTER ORANGE PEEL

BLACK COCK—a game bird native to Sweden

BROWNING or KITCHEN BOUQUET

CARAWAY SEED

CARDAMUM (also from the druggist, but more expensive)

CRAYFISH BUTTER

FENNEL (IN BOTTLES) [1] or substitute DILL

FENNEL SEED

GOLDEN SYRUP—dark corn syrup

NETTLES are available at leading stores. Spinach or dandelion greens may be substituted

POTATO FLOUR

RYE FLOUR

SAFFRON (also from the druggist, but more expensive)

SMOKED EEL (for sandwiches, or for the *smörgåsbord*)

SWEDISH ANCHOVIES AND HERRINGS

SWEDISH AQUAVIT (appetizer), and Swedish PUNSCH, are sold by leading wine merchants

SWEDISH CAVIAR (for sandwiches)

SWEDISH HARD BREAD (Various kinds)

---

[1] Fennel imparts such delicious flavor to many dishes that I advise anybody who owns a kitchen garden to grow this plant. It will thrive in any soil.

178

INDEX

A

B

Scandinavian Cookbooks

THE BEST OF FINNISH COOKING
by Taimi Previdi

200 easy-to-follow recipes covering all courses of the meal, along with menu suggestions for the major holidays and festivities like Mayday and Midsummer. Some of the classic Finnish recipes include Beef Lindstrom, Glassbowers Herring, Beer Soup, Cardamom Coffee Braid, and Lemon-flavored Mead.
242 pages, 0-7818-0284-9 (354) $19.95hc
COMING SOON IN PAPERBACK

THE BEST OF SMORGASBORD COOKING

The traditional Swedish smorgasbord, a large table of hot and cold dishes, is meant to be a selection of appetizers eaten before a seated dinner. *The Best of Smorgasbord Cooking* includes recipes for meat and game dishes, salads, fish, pasta and vegetables, and tips for garnishing and serving the dishes. These savory tidbits may be served in any combination or, when served alone, make excellent luncheon or supper dishes.
250 pages, 0-7818-0407-8 (207) $14.95pb

Scandinavian Dictionaries

FINNISH-ENGLISH COMPREHENSIVE DICTIONARY
80,000 entries
0-7818-0380-2 (467) $24.95hc

**FINNISH-ENGLISH/ENGLISH-FINNISH
CONCISE DICTIONARY**
12,000 entries
0-87052-813-0 (142) $11.95pb

**ICELANDIC-ENGLISH/ENGLISH-ICELANDIC
CONCISE DICTIONARY**
10,000 entries
0-87052-801-7 (147) $8.95pb

**NORWEGIAN-ENGLISH/ENGLISH-NORWEGIAN
CONCISE DICTIONARY**
5,000 entries
0-7818-0199-0 (202) $14.95pb

SWEDISH-ENGLISH COMPREHENSIVE DICTIONARY
900 pages
0-7818-0462-0 (437) $60.00hc

**SWEDISH-ENGLISH/ENGLISH-SWEDISH
STANDARD DICTIONARY**
70,000 entries
0-7818-0379-9 (242) $19.95pb

SWEDISH HANDY DICTIONARY
120 pages
0-87052-054-7 (345) $8.95pb

Coming Soon . . .
**ENGLISH-SWEDISH COMPREHENSIVE
ICELANDIC-ENGLISH COMPREHENSIVE
ENGLISH-ICELANDIC COMPREHENSIVE**

TREASURY OF FINNISH LOVE POEMS,QUOTATIONS & PROVERBS
in Finnish & English

edited by Börje Vähämäki

A bilingual collection of romantic imagery, including excerpts from the epic *Kalevala*, and its companion, the *Kanteletax*. Also included are modern works by Eeva Kilpi and Alexis Kivi, and selections in Swedish—the minority tongue of Finland—from Johann Ludwig Runeberg and Edith Sodergran.

128 pages, 5 x 7 inches
ISBN 0-7818-0397-7
$11.95 clothbound (118)

Coming Soon . . .

TREASURY OF FINNISH LOVE audiobook

HIPPOCRENE HANDY DICTIONARIES

For the traveler of independent spirit and curious mind, this practical series will help you to communicate, not just to get by.

All titles: 120 pages, 5" x 7", $8.95 paper

ARABIC
0463 • 0-87052-960-9

CHINESE
0347 • 0-87052-050-4

DUTCH
0323 • 0-87052-049-0

FRENCH
0155 • 0-7818-0010-2

GERMAN
0378 • 0-7818-0014-5

GREEK
0464 • 0-87052-961-7

ITALIAN
0196 • 0-7818-0011-0

JAPANESE
0466 • 0-87052-962-5

KOREAN
0438 • 0-7818-0082-X

PORTUGUESE
0324 • 0-87052-053-9

RUSSIAN
0371 • 0-7818-0013-7

SERBO-CROATIAN
0328 • 0-87052-051-2

SLOVAK
0359 • 0-7818-0101-X
* *$12.95*

SPANISH
0189 • 0-7818-0012-9

SWEDISH
0345 • 0-87052-054-7

THAI
0468 • 0-87052-963-3

TURKISH
0375 • 0-87052-982-X

(All prices subject to change.)
TO PURCHASE HIPPOCRENE BOOKS contact your local bookstore, or write to: HIPPOCRENE BOOKS, 171 Madison Avenue, New York, NY 10016. Please enclose check or money order, adding $5.00 shipping (UPS) for the first book and $.50 for each additional book.

HIPPOCRENE MASTERING SERIES

This teach-yourself language series, now available in 10 languages, is perfect for the serious traveler, student or businessperson.

MASTERING ARABIC
0-87052-922-6   (501)
$14.95pb
2 Cassettes
0-87052-984-6   (507) $12.95

MASTERING FINNISH
0-7818-0233-4   (184)
$14.95pb
2 Cassettes
0-7818-0265-2   (231) $12.95

MASTERING FRENCH
0-87052-055-5   (511)
$11.95pb
2 Cassettes
0-87052-060-1   (512) $12.95

MASTERING GERMAN
0-87052-056-3   (514)
$11.95pb
2 Cassettes
0-87052-061-X   (515) $12.95

MASTERING ITALIAN
0-87052-057-1   (517)
$11.95pb
2 Cassettes
0-87052-066-0   (521) $12.95

MASTERING JAPANESE
0-87052-923-4   (523)
$14.95pb
2 Cassettes
0-87052-983-8   (524) $12.95

MASTERING NORWE-GIAN
0-7818-0320-9   (472)
$14.95pb

MASTERING POLISH
0-7818-0015-3   (381)
$14.95pb
2 Cassettes
0-7818-0016-1   (389) $12.95

MASTERING RUSSIAN
0-7818-0270-9   (11)
$14.95pb
2 Cassettes
0-7818-0271-7   (13) $12.95

MASTERING SPANISH
0-87052-059-8   (527)
$11.95pb
2 Cassettes
0-87052-067-9   (528) $12.95

All prices subject to change. TO PURCHASE HIPPOCRENE BOOKS, contact your local bookstore, or write to: HIPPOCRENE BOOKS, 171 Madison Avenue, New York, NY 10016. Please enclose check or money order, adding $5.00 shipping (UPS) for the first book and $.50 for each additional book.